The power of the image

The power of the image

Essays on representation and sexuality

First published in 1985
by Routledge & Kegan Paul Ltd
Reprinted 1987

Reprinted in 1992, 1994 by
Routledge
11 New Fetter Lane, London EC4P 4EE
29 West 35th Street, New York, NY 10001

Set in Palatino 10pt
by Columns, Reading
and printed in Great Britain
by T.J. Press (Padstow) Ltd, Padstow, Cornwall

Library of Congress Cataloging in Publication Data

Kuhn, Annette

The power of the image.
Bibliography: p.
Includes index.
1. Feminism and motion pictures—Addresses,
essays, lecturers.   2. Women in moving pictures—
Addresses, essays, lectures.   I. Title.
PN1995.9W6K79 1985   791.43'01'5   85-1933

British Library CIP data also available

ISBN 0–415–08460–1 (pbk)

Contents

Acknowledgments

The essays in this book were written over a period of some five or six years and, in the course of their production, I have enjoyed the assistance of numerous people and institutions. With individual chapters, acknowledgments of assistance appear in the appropriate Notes and References: here there is space only to say a general 'thank you' to all who helped over the years in this work. In putting together the essays as a book, I have been greatly assisted by Sarah Montgomery, who did wordprocessing and provided friendship and encouragement; by Jim Adams of the BFI Education Department, who produced many of the illustrations; and by Philippa Brewster, Helen Armitage and Helen Mott of Routledge & Kegan Paul, who have been unfailingly supportive.

Chapter 1, 'Living dolls and "real women" ' is reprinted courtesy of *Camerawork* and Frances Borzello, Jill Pack and Cassandra Wedd. Chapter 4 is a revised version of *'The Big Sleep*: a disturbance in the sphere of sexuality', which appeared in *Wide Angle*, vol.4, no.3, 1980, © Johns Hopkins University Press. Photographs are reproduced courtesy of The Kobal Collection, Lee Friedlander, M-G-M and the Samuelson Family Archive. Stills are from films produced by Paramount, Warner Brothers and the Samuelson Film Company. The authors and publishers are also grateful to the British Film Institute for permission to reproduce photographs 3.1 and 5.1 from The National Film Archive.

Extracts from Crown-copyright records in the Public Record Office appear by permission of the Controller of Her Majesty's Stationery Office.

Introduction

The twentieth century's second wave of Western feminism has distinguished itself from other social and political movements in several important respects. Its espousal of non-hierarchical approaches to organisation and action have lent themselves particularly well to issue-oriented politics – campaigns around abortion legislation and direct action on peace and disarmament, for example. The movement's insistence on bringing to centre stage areas of life hitherto considered secondary, even irrelevant, to 'serious' politics – the division of labour in the household, relations between men and women at home and in the workplace, emotions, sexuality, even the Unconscious – also sets it apart, giving ground to a conviction that the women's movement is opening up and beginning to explore a whole new country. In this process, new maps have had to be drawn, concepts constructed, systems of thought developed, in the effort to order the apparent chaos of a neglected other side of patriarchal culture. To take just one example of the effects of all this: trade union campaigns to combat sexual harassment at work would have been inconceivable before the middle or late 1970s, if only because the phenomenon simply did not have a name before that time. One can scarcely organise around a non-existent concept.

In other words, politics and knowledge are interdependent. In the ordinary way, the link between them will often go unnoticed or be taken for granted: where feminism is concerned, however, this is impossible, precisely because knowledge has had to be self-consciously produced alongside political activity. Each has regenerated the other. This is not to imply that the relationship is always a harmonious and uncontradictory one: mutual dependency always involves difficulty and struggle. Feminists may disagree, for example, on the extent to which producing knowledge is in itself a political activity. Are theory and practice in the final instance separate categories? Or is it acceptable to posit (to use a currently rather unfashionable term) a 'theoretical practice' of feminism?

Knowledge of the kind likely to be useful to the women's movement – knowledge, that is, which increases our understanding of women's lives and the institutions and structures of power which impinge on those lives in varying degrees and in different ways, structures which construct woman as 'other' in a patriarchal society – much of this knowledge is being produced under the banner of women's studies. The fact that women's studies has come to assume an existence in the Academy, apparently independent of the women's movement, may present some problems for the relationship between a body of knowledge and the movement which was its initial *raison d'être*. However, precisely because it so evidently eschews the 'neutrality' demanded by the Academy, the status of women's studies as a subject, researched and taught in universities, polytechnics and colleges, is marginal and precarious and its future uncertain: women's studies, therefore, needs the women's movement as much as *vice versa*. Women's studies also needs an institutional space to develop, and it needs, as well, the opportunity to draw on other areas of intellectual endeavour where these promise to be useful and relevant to its project. The saying that knowledge does not come from nowhere has more than one meaning.

Which brings me to the subject of this book. From its beginnings, feminism has regarded ideas, language and images as crucial in shaping women's (and men's) lives. In the USA in 1968, feminists staged a demonstration against

2

the Miss America contest, protesting the event on grounds that it promoted an impossible image of ideal womanhood, and was complicit in the widespread idea that all women – not only participants in beauty contests – are reducible to a set of bodily attributes. From this beginning there followed critiques of stereotypical representations of women in advertisements and in films, and studies of the ways in which language – both vocabulary and linguistic usage – defines and confines women. From the point of view of its politics, then, the women's movement has always been interested in images, meanings, representations – and especially in challenging representations which, while questionable or offensive from a feminist standpoint, are from other points of view – if they are noticed at all – perfectly acceptable.

This interest is in part responsible for the chapters in the present book. I say responsible, because without the women's movement a desire to question representation in this way could not be articulated, nor would the public or even the private space to do so exist. I say in part, however, because since the early days feminist interest in images and representations has taken a variety of forms and directions. These have been determined largely by different ways in which representation has been thought about and analysed – that is, by the theories and methods brought to bear on the question. The question, I would argue, is a feminist one: the theories and methods not exclusively so. These come, at least to begin with, from elsewhere, and are appropriated and adapted to the feminist project. Knowledge does not come from nowhere, then: just as in this instance new knowledge is generated through the desire of feminist politics, so existing knowledge is both used and transformed in the service of this desire. The use and transformation of existing knowledge also partly motivates this book, then. It does not pretend to offer a comprehensive account of feminist thought on representation, however, but rather limits itself to an in-depth exploration of certain theoretical and methodological paths, hopefully opening up one or two new byways in the process. Which paths, though, and why?

The emergence of a new feminist movement in the late 1960s coincided with a renewed interest in marxist thought on 'the superstructure' – ideas, culture, ideology – and the place and effectivity of the superstructure within the social formation.[1] The different terms used here to describe the contents of the superstructure reflect a range of tendencies within marxist theory. Certain developments around the concept of ideology, for instance, were embodied in the work of the French philosopher Louis Althusser, work which – alongside that of other intellectuals, Roland Barthes and Claude Lévi-Strauss, for instance – was associated with structuralism. Barthes had written an introduction to semiotics – the study of signification, or meaning production, in society – and his book *Mythologies* comprised a series of short semiotically-informed essays on specific images and representations, and on signification in general: which elements in images produce meaning, how the process operates, and so on.[2]

In the early 1970s, art historian John Berger made a series of programmes for BBC Television called *Ways of Seeing*. In these, Berger also considered how images make meaning, though in this instance without explicit recourse to semiotic concepts. Into this effectively semiotic project Berger injected a more orthodoxly marxist concern with the status of images as commodities – artifacts which are bought and sold, which have exchange value. One particularly influential programme dealt with the female nude, both in the European high art tradition and in mass-produced pinup photographs. Analysis dealt not only with the formal qualities of these images *per se*, but also with the relationship between images and their consumers – who as well as being spectators are often buyers/owners of images too.

Althusserian thought had a certain relevance to feminism because it contained a notion that human beings are constructed by ideology, that our ways of thinking about the world, of representing it to ourselves, becomes so 'naturalised' that we take our conception of that world for granted. If ideology effaces itself, the process by which this takes place could, for instance, explain (though Althusser did not in fact attempt to do so) the taken-for-granted nature of social constructs of femininity. Barthes's work on images suggested, moreover, that meanings are produced through the codes at work in representations, and that while meanings might appear to be natural, obvious, immanent, they are in fact produced: they are constructed through identifiable processes of signification at work in all representations. Finally, *Ways of Seeing* showed that meaning production takes place within social and historical contexts, and that in a capitalist society representations are no more exempt than any other products from considerations of the marketplace.

It is not difficult to see a potential for crossfertilisation between these ideas and feminist concerns with representation: indeed, the work I have described forms a backcloth to the chapters in this book. It is really no more than a backcloth, though. Since the early 1970s, the study of images, particularly of cinematic images, as signifying systems has taken up and developed these 'prefeminist' concerns, bringing to the fore the issue of the spectator as subject addressed, positioned, even formed, by representations. To semiotic and structuralist approaches to representation has been added psychoanalysis, whose object is precisely the processes by which human subjectivity is formed.[3] In work on the image, the cinematic image particularly, an emphasis on subjectivity has foregrounded the question of spectatorship in new ways. This, too, informs the writing in this book.

But again, that is by no means the whole story: for feminist thought has long since entered the field of representation in its own right. These chapters may be read as inhabiting a tradition of feminist work on representation which draws strategically on the strands of non-feminist or prefeminist thinking I have described, if only because their objects (images, meanings, ideologies) and their objectives (analysis, deconstruction) have something in common with feminist concerns. At the same time, though, the very process of appropriation has exposed crucial weaknesses in these systems of thought – notably gender-blindness, formalism, and certain methodological shortcomings.[4] Not only, though, has the appropriation of pre-existing theory necessarily – and fruitfully – produced criticisms of it: the particular concerns of feminism, when mapped onto that theory, have been instrumental in generating qualitatively new knowledge, in constructing a new field.

Inevitably, the questions addressed in these chapters traverse both feminist concerns and knowledge-in-process. What relation, for instance, does spectatorship have to representations of women? What sort of activity is looking? What does looking have to do with sexuality? With masculinity and femininity? With power? With knowledge? How do images of women in particular, 'speak to' the spectator? Is the spectator addressed as male/female, masculine/feminine? Is femininity constructed in specific ways through representation? Why are images of women's bodies so prevalent in our society? Such questions may sometimes be answered by looking at and analysing actual images. But although such analysis must be regarded as necessary to an understanding of the relationship between representation and sexuality, it is not always sufficient. For, in practice, images are always seen in context: they always have a specific use value in the particular time and place of their consumption. This, together with their formal characteristics, conditions and limits the meanings available from them at any one moment. But if representations always have use value, then more often than not they also have exchange value: they circulate as commodities in a social/economic system. This further conditions, or overdetermines, the meanings available from representations.

Meanings do not reside in images, then: they are circulated between representation, spectator and social formation. All of the chapters in this book are concerned in one way or another with images – with films as well as still photographs of various kinds. Each chapter places a slightly different emphasis on each of the terms defining the representation-spectator-social formation triangle: though, given the central place accorded the instance of looking, the spectator undoubtedly sits at the apex. Nevertheless, each chapter marks a move further away from the model of the image/text as an isolated object of analysis, and closer to a conception of the image as inhabiting various contexts: cultural contexts of spectatorship, institutional and social/ historical contexts of production and consumption. At the same time, conceptualising texts as embedded within a series of contextual layers, and trying to do this without losing sight of texts as productive of meaning in their own right, does produce certain theoretical and methodological difficulties. These are touched on here and there throughout the book, and are explicitly discussed in the introductions to the final two chapters, in which attempts are made theoretically and methodologically to handle texts and contexts in tandem.

All of the texts/images discussed in these chapters may, in a broad sense, be regarded as 'culturally dominant'. Most of them – Hollywood films and softcore pornography, for example – are produced commercially for mass audiences. Where this is not the case, as with some of the photographs discussed in Chapter 1, they strive to slot into hegemonic 'high art' institutions. Hegemony is never without contradiction, however, which is one reason why analysing culturally dominant representations can be very productive. Contextual overdetermination notwithstanding, meaning can never be finally guaranteed. In practice, the operations of texts and various levels of context are rarely in harmony, and there is always some space for 'aberrant' reception of dominant representations. One of the essays (Chapter 5) attempts to trace the processes through which such readings of a group of films became possible at a particular historical moment. More generally, the very existence of a book like this one is testimony to the fact that readings 'against the grain' are not only available, but often compelling. The activity of deconstruction sets loose an array of 'unintended' meanings, by their nature subversive of the apparently transparent meanings which texts offer us.

But why spend time and effort analysing images of a kind often considered questionable, even objectionable, by feminists? Why not try instead to create alternatives to culturally dominant representations? As I have argued, politics and knowledge are interdependent: the women's movement is not, I believe, faced here with a choice between two mutually exclusive alternatives, though individual feminists – if only because one person's life is too short to encompass everything – often experience their own politics in such a way. Theory and practice inform one another. At one level, analysing and deconstructing dominant representations may be regarded as a strategic practice. It produces understanding, and understanding is necessary to action.

It may also be considered an act of resistance in itself. Politics is often thought of as one of life's more serious undertakings, allowing little room for pleasure. At the same time, feminists may feel secretly guilty about their enjoyment of images they are convinced ought to be rejected as politically unsound. In analysing such images, though, it is possible, indeed necessary, to acknowledge their pleasurable qualities, precisely because pleasure is an area of analysis in its own right. 'Naive' pleasure, then, becomes admissible. And the acts of analysis, of deconstruction and of reading 'against the grain' offer an additional pleasure – the pleasure of resistance, of saying 'no': not to 'unsophisticated' enjoyment, by ourselves and others, of culturally dominant images, but to the structures of power which ask us to consume them uncritically and in highly circumscribed ways.

1

Living dolls and 'real women'

Frances Borzello, Annette Kuhn, Jill Pack
and Cassandra Wedd

The writers of this chapter were among a group of feminists who met over a period of time in the late 1970s to share a common interest in photographs – in making as much as in talking about them. Looking at images in magazines and advertisements, discussing each others' pictures, setting up joint photographic projects, our efforts were largely informal, low-key and private. The group, which eventually acquired the name Second Sight, provided an opportunity to pool ideas and develop skills in circumstances free of the pressures to get things done, to produce results, which all of its members faced in one way or another in our everyday lives. The group did, however (not without hesitation, given the exploratory and informal nature of our activities), once or twice venture onto more public terrain. This collectively-written chapter was the result of one such venture.

It deals with some photographs of women which, as well as possessing exchange value in particular markets, also circulate a currency of codes through which 'woman' is constructed in representation. In this sense, the chapter picks up on Second Sight's broad concern, as a group of feminists, with trying to understand how 'mainstream' photographic images work, how women are represented, how femininity is constructed, within them. Some of the issues touched on here – notably questions of spectatorship, of looking – find an echo in other chapters in this book. The

9

specificity of this chapter, though, is its concern with certain conventions, particular genres, of still photography – notably glamour photography, the nude and documentary photography – and how these are expressed and reworked not only through individual images, but through sets of images whose meanings are crucially bound up in their particular forms of commodification. Meanings readable from photographs, in other words, are at all points connected with the status they occupy as products, with the contexts of reception and discourses of authorship, aesthetics, criticism and marketing which surround them. 'Mainstream' images in our culture bear the traces of the capitalist and patriarchal social relations in which they are produced, exchanged and consumed.

Given this, why should feminists be interested in looking at, in analysing, such images? For Second Sight, such a project was certainly felt to be of some use in relation to our own individual, collective and private activities as makers of photographs. It has relevance also to a broader, more public, feminist cultural politics, however: to what is described in this chapter as 'our practice as producers of images of ourselves'. The implication is that in order to challenge dominant representations, it is necessary first of all to understand how they work, and thus where to seek points of possible productive transformation. From such under-standing flow various politics and practices of oppositional cultural production, among which may be counted feminist interventions. But perhaps there is another justification for a feminist analysis of mainstream images of women: may it not teach us to recognise inconsistencies and contradictions within dominant traditions of representation, to identify points of leverage for our own intervention: cracks and fissures through which may be captured glimpses of what might in other circumstances be possible, visions of 'a world outside the order not normally seen or thought about'?

Whenever we look at painted, drawn, sculpted or photo-graphed images of women, it is important for us to remind ourselves that images of women have traditionally been

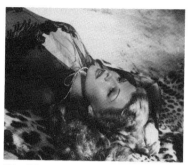

Rita Hayworth, 1942

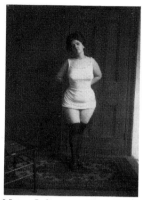

New Orleans, about 1912

the province and property of men.[1] Today our reading of these images must inevitably be informed by this insight, itself hard won in women's struggle towards consciousness and autonomy. However, to hold exclusively to an awareness of the male hegemony of representations of woman is to set aside critical awareness of variations within this broad tradition, some of which may well turn out to be useful, even if negatively, in determining our practice as producers of images of ourselves. It is particularly difficult to make critical distinctions in that area of representation that takes women's sexuality as its topic.

It is by now a commonplace that the transformation of the unclothed woman from being naked to being nude (one of the major 'achievements' of the European high art tradition) also brings about, in all forms of representation, the transformation of woman into object, the site of structures both of exchange and of looking. The spectator is the buyer, the buyer is the spectator.[2] To possess a woman's sexuality is to possess the woman; to possess the image of a woman's sexuality is, however mass-produced the image, also in some way to possess, to maintain a degree of control over, woman in general. In this situation the female spectator of images of women has until very recently been faced with a single option – to identify with the male in the spectator and to see woman, to see herself, as an object of desire.

Glamour, a notion applied almost exclusively to women, takes this process one step further. Glamour is understood generally to imply a sense of deceptive fascination, of groomed beauty, of charm enhanced by means of illusion. A glamorous/glamourised image then is one manipulated, falsified perhaps, in order to heighten or even to idealise. A glamorous image of a woman (or an image of a glamorous woman) is peculiarly powerful in that it plays on the desire of the spectator in a particularly pristine way: beauty or sexuality is desirable exactly to the extent that it is idealised and unattainable.

The crudeness of the relations of exchange and ownership which underpin a simple representation of the female nude is rendered more subtle and more powerful to the degree that the image is idealised. This is not, of course, to suggest that there are no glamorous nude images, on the contrary. But it is important to hold to this distinction between the glamour portrait and the nude since it enables us to pinpoint differences in the ways in which images of women work for us. Indeed, the distinction is a particularly useful (though not the only) one to be made in considering the very different images of women presented in books of photographs such as, on the one hand, E.J. Bellocq's *Storyville Portraits*, and on the other, the *Hollywood Glamor Portraits* (though this book does also include pictures of men).[3]

In a sense, the Hollywood portraits are much easier to deal with than Bellocq's photographs. Apart from the fact of their obvious provenance in the commercial film industry in the days of its ascendance, the 1930s and 1940s, they are immediately recognisable in aesthetic terms as part of that tradition of images of women which include – as well as publicity portraits of film stars – images of women in certain types of advertising and pinups of the glossy *Playboy/Penthouse* genre. It is no coincidence that the glamourised woman is particularly strongly represented in mass-produced, as opposed to traditional high art, images: the desire invoked by the idealised/unattainable 'glamour girl' reflects only too accurately the real unattainability, certainly, of the woman so represented, and also – and in many ways more importantly – of the image of perfection that glamour pictures offer.

12

The Playgirl of the Month may evoke masturbatory fantasies in the male spectator, it is true: for us as women, though, the perfectly beautiful film stars of the 1930s and 1940s and the perfectly beautiful women in the glossy clothes and cosmetic ads of today hold out a vision of perfection which few of us can ever attain. The desire for such perfection which, even while we love the movies of Garbo, Hayworth and others, we may well realise is hopeless, is to be displaced onto desire for the products they advertise or connote. As far as the film industry is concerned, to place the consumer of the films themselves in a constant position of desire is to bring him or her back to the cinema time and time again, to seek an unattainable fantasy life. The star system, founded crucially on idealised images of women, constitutes those images as commodities which would, in a self-perpetuating cycle, generate further relations of exchange and increased profitability. Women's bodies and selling were identified: representations of women became the commodities that film producers were able to exchange in return for money.

A good deal of the groomed beauty of the women of the glamour portraits comes from the fact that they are 'made-up', in the immediate sense that cosmetics have been applied to their bodies in order to enhance their existing qualities. But they are also 'made-up' in the sense that the images, rather than the women, are put together, constructed, even fabricated or falsified in the sense that we might say a story is made up if it is a fiction. The wordplay is revealing. Glamour is in many ways about surface appearances: the expressionistic lighting of the Hollywood portraits – especially when looked at in relation to codes at work in certain films of the period (those of Lang, Ophuls and Cukor to name only three directors, many of whose films were, significantly, considered by the industry to be aimed primarily at a female audience) – with its play of light, shadow and texture, serves quite succinctly to demonstrate this.

Glamour photography is very much open to the criticism that, at the same time as it holds out idealised images, in particular of women, it also promotes the ideal woman as being put together, composed of surfaces and defined by appearance. It is here that the glamour tradition in all its manifestations may be seen to occupy a place dangerously close to another tradition of representation of women, from myth to fairytale to high art to pornography, in which they are stripped of will and autonomy. Woman is dehumanised by being represented as a kind of automaton, a 'living doll': *The Sleeping Beauty, Coppélia, L'Histoire d'O*, 'She's a real doll!'

Freud illustrated his essay on 'The Uncanny' with reference to the tale of the living doll Olympia in Hoffman's *Nachtstücken*[4]: stories of this kind can evoke a real sense of unease. *The Stepford Wives* (1974, directed by Bryan Forbes), an otherwise unexceptional film, in which the women of a small Connecticut community are taken over by an alien force and turned into robots which service their husbands unquestioningly, was carefully marketed and widely reviewed in Britain as a film with feminist interest. This was precisely because of its mobilisation of the real fear women have of seeing ourselves in terms of what may be a male fantasy of control over our labour power and sexuality and our terror of becoming transformed according to that fantasy. It also suggests the potential threat to male sexuality posed by female desire.

The representations of women in David Hamilton's *Dreams of Young Girls* photographs, which are quite evidently contemporary instances of the glamour tradition, may be seen as an attempt to neutralise the potentially threatening aspects of mature female sexuality by eroticising the immature, barely sexual, sexuality of pubescent girls. No doubt the mass distribution and sale of postcard reproductions of these photographs, the popularity of Hamilton's two films, and the appearance in the late 1970s of a spate of movies dealing with child prostitution, are all significant in this respect: it is often said that nowadays the film industry cannot cope with 'real women'.

The coincidence by which Hamilton's postcards and prints happened to be on display alongside Bellocq's in an exhibition at The Photographers' Gallery in London of the

Storyville Portraits is instructive as well as ironic. The apparent similarity of their subject matter scarcely masks their real dissimilarities, which are by no means solely the difference between the 1970s and 1912. Hamilton's work falls squarely within the glamour tradition of representations of women, a tradition which seems to have assumed a degree of dominance, certainly where mass-produced photographic images of women are concerned. However, even though within the male hegemony over women's image traditions other than this do exist, applying the labels 'documentary' or 'realist' to photographs such as Bellocq's does not necessarily explain them, either.

Part of the problem is the subtitle of the book of Bellocq's photographs. It describes them as pictures of New Orleans prostitutes taken around 1912, thus perhaps raising expectations of a work documenting hitherto unavailable information. Yet it is exceedingly difficult to locate precisely where in these photos the documentary element resides. One reason for the difficulty is that stylistically they do not fit into any existing pattern of prostitute pictures. Toulouse-Lautrec's 1896 colour lithograph series *Elles* suggests (to the spectator) forbidden information, with its rumpled beds and hints of affection between prostitutes. Degas' art, while not of prostitutes, shares a similar concern to reproduce the intimate, and shows women at their most private, and by implication, their most natural, in the tub or brushing their hair. His pastel paintings of nudes submitted to the last Impressionist show in 1886 caused an outrage, and his women were likened to cats licking themselves. 'The nude', he told George Moore, 'has always been represented in poses which presuppose an audience, but these women of mine are honest, simple folk, unconcerned by any other interest than those involved in their physical condition. . . . It is as if you look through a keyhole.'[5] Brassai, photographing in the 1930s, gives a factual, but normally private, view of prostitute and client dressing themselves after the act. In all three cases, the women are presented as unaware of the artist, a classic technique for convincing the spectator of the documentary truth of what is seen.

15

Bellocq's prostitutes, by contrast, are posed. They collude with the camera, staring at it, smiling at it, acting coy for it, or proud. The product of such behaviour could rightly be expected to be an erotic photograph. Yet the erotic is not the strongest element in these pictures, even though in our culture representations of unclothed women often hold immediate sexual overtones. When nudity or nakedness can be held to be a legitimate documentary element, the line between revelation and display is indeed fine, and the distinction becomes that much more difficult to hold to when the subject of documentation bears connotations of illicit sexual activity.

If only because we do not really know why Bellocq made his portraits of New Orleans prostitutes, it is especially difficult to approach his work. Are the pictures titillating ones by a dirty old man who was able to gain access to brothels by means of his camera, the tool of his voyeurism? Or were they perhaps straight commercial portraits, commissioned by the women themselves or by the madams of their brothels to show to potential employers or clients? Neither of these explanations seems really satisfactory.

However, perhaps exactly because we are able to approach Bellocq's work without the straitjacket of preconceived categories, our reading can be informed by an unusual and possibly productive degree of openness: because Bellocq's intentions provide us with no clues, all we have to go on is the photographs themselves. Indeed, why should our understanding of these photographs be prefaced by knowing the intentions of the photographer? No reading of a picture can be unambiguous, or completely objective. Even knowing a photographer's intentions should not prevent the viewer of the photograph from contributing to the information that the photograph emits.

What is immediately striking about these photographs is their variety. The women are posed against different backgrounds and are in varying degrees clothed or unclothed. A minority are completely naked. The frankness of the women in relation to the camera, and the very variety of the poses, suggests that the images might well be of the women's own choosing rather than reflections of the photographer's obsessions. Their documentary quality seems therefore to come at least as much from the subjects themselves as from the photographer, a point which is underscored by a comparison between these photographs and the coy soft-pornography of the same period: the women who are unclothed are more often than not naked rather than nude.

In general, the way in which they wear, or do not wear, their clothes constitutes the mark of their professional status as women whose sexuality is attainable – as opposed, that is, to the unattainability of the sexuality of the glamour nude. It is perhaps in this sense that the photographs may be given the label documentary, although it is a reflection of our puzzlement in the face of such unusual (unreadable) photographs of women that the picture chosen for the cover of the book is among the handful out of the whole collection which does actually cross the boundary between documentary and glamour.

To approach them as images of women is not the only way in which the Storyville and Hollywood portraits can be read, however. These photos also exist as 'art'. The Storyville prints are collected for their quality of uniqueness, for the buyers' knowledge that the reproductions are from originals found in a drawer decades after they were taken. The Hollywood portraits, though mass-produced and therefore, one might think, outside the realm of 'art', are collected for their nostalgia value, an artistically respectable category for assigning monetary value to the ephemera of times past. It is striking that, despite their different modes of production, the grounds for elevating these photographs to art – their aesthetic quality – are shared by both. The technical perfection of the Hollywood photos and the surreal quality imparted to the Storyville prints by the effects of ageing and the scratched-out parts of certain images provide the aesthetic justification for legitimising their sale as prints at £20 (Hollywood) and £100 (Storyville).

As far as content is concerned there is perhaps no threat for women in the way the market turns the Hollywood photos into art, their role as 'advertisements' for the motion picture industry now being widely understood. But the elevation of the Storyville pictures into art gives rise to some unease. In representing the women sympathetically, they show a world outside the order normally seen or thought about. Can their transformation into art objects be seen as assimilating and containing this quality of 'otherness', which might really be a challenge to accepted ways of seeing women?

2

Lawless seeing

Representations are productive: photographs, far from merely reproducing a pre-existing world, constitute a highly coded discourse which, among other things, constructs whatever is in the image as object of consumption – consumption by looking, as well as often quite literally by purchase. It is no coincidence, therefore, that in many highly socially visible (and profitable) forms of photography women dominate the image. Where photography takes women as its subject matter, it also constructs 'woman' as a set of meanings which then enter cultural and economic circulation on their own account. Women appear in many types of photography: the glamour portraits of women movie stars and the quasi-documentary pictures of early twentieth-century prostitutes looked at in the last chapter are only two of many categories, each one constructing a different type of woman. Cultural meanings centred on the signifier 'woman' may become relatively fixed in use: but a certain range of meaning is still available.

It is true (if somewhat reductive) to say that in a patriarchal culture most representations of women are readable as connoting 'otherness' or difference – difference from the norm of patriarchy, that is. The fact that they do this in distinct and often contradictory ways in various media, genres and contexts is an important justification for the practice of analysing and deconstructing culturally dominant images. Pornography is of particular interest here because, in its frank obsession with sex, its construction of sexual difference is relatively transparent. The production of woman as 'other' demands that pornography speak both to and from a masculine subject position. This chapter explores the question of how certain widely-used forms of pornography (the argument restricts itself mainly to pinups and softcore, venturing only briefly and tentatively into a consideration of hardcore and violent pornography) construct femininity and female sexuality as objects of obsessively repetitive investigation by spectator/consumers whose desire to fathom these mysteries is constantly being evoked.

Writing about pornography holds particular hazards for a feminist. This chapter was written originally for a book, subsequently abandoned, on pornography. The project was an impossible one, for a variety of personal/political reasons. For one thing, pornography seems to exert an almost obsessive lure which has accorded it a place in feminist politics more central, in my view, than it deserves. At the same time, analysing porn lacks the pleasurability afforded by considering, say, publicity photos of film stars. After several months of work on the book, it became increasingly difficult to deal with images which seemed crude, tasteless and unimaginative in the extreme: though the fact that I did like some pinups in the glossier, upmarket men's magazines suggests that some degree of class-based aesthetic judgement may have been at work in my distaste for the rest. But not simply that, I think.

For me, looking at pornography and analysing its appeal to a certain type of masculinity produced the view, paradoxically perhaps, that if anything in our culture is unfathomable, it is masculinity itself. Which raises the question of the status, for a feminist, of a project of analysing pornographic images. Might such an activity not turn out, in a sense, to mirror porn's address to its male consumers – framing a desire to get to the bottom of something one does not understand? Except that in this case it is obviously not femininity that is at issue. Such desires, of course, are perfect parallels of the quest for knowledge. But at the same time, the capacity of pornography to provoke gut reactions – of distaste, horror, sexual arousal, fear – makes it peculiarly difficult to deal with analytically. In the first place, the intellectual distance necessary for analysis becomes hard to sustain: and also feminist (and indeed any other) politics around pornography tend to acquire a degree of emotionalism that can make the enterprise quite explosive. Any feminist who ventures to write about pornography puts herself in an exposed position, therefore.

Another good reason for hesitation is the very complexity of the questions pornography raises, the difficulty of constructing, distinguishing and sustaining positions, and so of producing coherent political programmes, on the issue. The widespread tendency for feminist arguments on pornography to be confused with those of rightwing moralists makes it especially important to insist upon certain distinctions. Arguments advanced in this chapter would perhaps suggest that, as both a regime of representation and an industry, pornography not only constructs woman, femininity and female sexuality in ways which feminists, women (and indeed men) have every right to object to: it is also in effect inimical to the very sexual liberation it purports to advocate. Nonetheless, it would be a mistake to move straight from this conclusion into a rhetoric of condemnation which, in reply to the insistent question of what should be done about pornography, resorts immediately to censorship: 'it ought to be banned'. On the contrary: this analysis implies not only that censorship of one kind or another is actually a condition of the effectiveness of certain types of pornography, but also that, in any case, censorship can in no way deal with the specific objections to pornography raised by a feminist analysis of how it works.

The question of what is to be done about pornography – however impertinent it may at first sight appear to be in relation to a project of deconstructing porn's strategies of address – cannot and should not be sidestepped. It may usefully be rephrased in the present context as an inquiry about the usefulness of the sort of analysis offered here. Such analysis can help clarify thinking in a notoriously

21

difficult and emotionally-charged area, an area in which questions of policy and political strategy are always particularly prominent. Moreover, the activity of analysis may be regarded as a strategy in its own right: it seems entirely appropriate, by deconstructing its operations, to debunk and demystify pornography. There is perhaps a certain pleasure, too, in taking issue with porn's inflated self-image as sexually liberating, and so radically shifting the terms of a discourse in which pornography is constructed, by its defenders and its moralist antagonists alike, as a distinct and privileged regime of representation.

A deconstruction of pornography makes it possible to handle the specificity and complexity of its different forms: its cultural variability, its diverse technologies and modes of production and consumption, its status as at once commodity, industry and representation. Such an approach also insists that pornography is not after all special, is not a privileged order of representation; that it shares many of its modes of address, many of its codes and conventions, with representations which are not looked upon as a 'problem' in the way pornography is. This has significant consequences for any feminist politics around pornography in particular and around representation in general. This essay cannot pretend to offer an exhaustive analysis: the issue is too complex for that. Nor does it set out any political programme. Clearly, there is more work to be done – though the political necessity and the utility of such work are questions that should always be kept in mind.

What does pornography do? What does it say? Who does it speak to? Where does it speak from? On one level, the contemporary pornography industry may be seen as part of a general trend to increased investment in, and consumption of, leisure goods and services, part of that tendency to promote privatised forms of rapid gratification which characterises late capitalism. Accepting this, though, many would nevertheless argue that what is specific about porn is its preoccupation with a certain subject matter: sex. Is this perhaps what makes pornography so engaging and yet so disturbing? Sexual passion and desire threaten the normal, the liveable, the everyday, with all manner of distraction. Socially, such a capacity to disrupt appears to call forth containment within conventions and institutions of hetero-sexual courtship, marriage, family. But a degree of excess perhaps remains to find expression in sexual fantasy – much of it taking entirely socially unacceptable forms. Is por-nography then a commodity through which sexual fantasy is evoked, constructed, circulated?

Whatever it does, pornography is, of course, exactly a commodity: it is produced, bought and sold. To the extent that porn participates in the disruptive potential of sexual passion, it is indeed dangerous merchandise. But in its attempt to articulate sexual fantasy through particular regimes of representation, pornography seeks at the same time to contain these very qualities of fascination and disrup-tion – in the process becoming literal, earnest, clinical. Porn is often, in consequence, profoundly disappointing to its con-sumers, whose dissatisfaction may well be one of the things that keeps the trade so buoyant: there is always the hope, after all, that it can be assuaged by trying (and buying) again. Although its users often say that pornography is repetitive and boring, it is obviously dangerous as well, since it has to be kept out of sight. In order to maintain its attraction, porn demands strictures, controls, censorship. Exposed to the light of day, it risks a loss of power. Pornography invites policing.

If pornography is about sex, there is nothing at all straightforward about that, either. In the first place, it is unlikely that porn is *only* about sex. Moreover, it works in highly specific ways, deploying particular modes of rep-resentation in particular social-historical contexts. In this chapter, I shall argue that crucial among the concerns of certain types of contemporary pornography is a construction, an assertion, of sexual difference. But if pornography participates in – reflects, conditions, constructs – contempor-ary Western discourses around sexuality and sexual differ-ence, it is by no means the only category of representation to do this. What I want to consider here, then, are some of the ways in which pornography, as a regime of representation, addresses a particular audience in a particular context, producing meanings pivoting on gender difference: and how in this process it constructs a social discourse on the nature of human sexuality.

The word pornography, a nineteeth-century coinage, referred originally to writings about the lives and activities of prostitutes. In its earliest sense, therefore, pornography was rather limited in its approach to the representation of sex and sexual activity. This link with prostitution gives pornography a lowlife cast, which must have produced a titillating association with the desirably/undesirably forbidden, the illicit, the underground, certainly for consumers of a particular social class. Despite the fact that pornography has existed under that name since about the mid-nineteenth century, and depictions of erotic and sexual activity have been around – even if not called pornography – from time immemorial, such representations are by no means homogeneous in terms either of their textual operations or of the cultural meanings they carried in the societies in which they were produced. The nature of, and readings available from, representations of sexual activity will vary according to their social-historical conditions of production and consumption. Among these, modes of production – and technologies of reproduction – of representations of all kinds, pornography included, are paramount. Developments in these areas over the past hundred years or so have been especially significant as regards pornography.

When the term pornography first came into use, virtually the only medium in which representations could be reproduced in very large numbers was print. The printed word demands literacy, and not everyone was able to read. As a written medium, pornography was consequently limited as to the audience it could reach, and seems to have been something of a gentleman's pastime. Porn did of course exist in visual media as well: but paintings and drawings also found a numerically small and socially exclusive market. Engravings and broadsheets, which did not call for literacy, were rather more widely circulated, but were still by no means a mass medium. Developments in techniques of mechanical reproduction of photographic images and consequently in the capacity to produce large quantities cheaply[1] opened up limitless horizons for pornographers. The apparent realism of the photographic image undoubtedly proved an added attraction for consumers, too. Mechanical reproduction of still photographic images, then, offered a breakthrough in the public availability of pornography. The advent of cheap, mass-produced visual pornography opened the market to the less well-off, foreign immigrants, the illiterate, the working classes.

Today, pornography using photographic reproduction and its variants is very much in the ascendant, while literary porn appeals only to a relatively limited market, attracting little in the way either of opprobrium or of censorship. Magazines and individual photographs deal in still images, while cinema – which entered the field of pornography early in its own history – adds movement and narrativity to the photographic image. Current growth media for pornography are television and video: porn users with the appropriate equipment can subscribe to cable-TV stations which broadcast nothing but softcore, or may rent or buy hardcore and softcore on videotape to view at home. Present-day pornography is produced across a range of media, from the printed word through to television, though the market is dominated by visual forms drawing on various conventions of photographic realism. As representation, porn also has genres and subgenres of its own, its own favourite themes and subject matters. In addition to mass-market pornography aimed at a relatively wide audience, parts of the porn trade also cater for sectional interests and minority sexual tastes.

At a certain point, therefore, it becomes difficult to talk in any but a very general way about how pornography works, even when investigation is confined to its contemporary Western variants. Each of the media in which pornography is produced makes meanings, addresses its consumers, in particular ways. Each constructs specific inflections of pornography's more general ideological operations. Nevertheless, it is possible to deconstruct and analyse these operations through readings of pornographic representations:

though it should be borne in mind that contexts of production and reception, just as much as formal features of texts, inform readings. For example, the reader of this chapter will (I assume) be approaching her or his understanding of pornography from rather a different angle than the average devotee of porn.

Probably the most widespread format in which pornography appears at present is still photographs, usually printed in books or magazines. Porn on videotape and, to a lesser extent, pornographic movies are also very popular, but their consumption requires hardware and/or premises which are not universally accessible. Pornographic photos, magazines and books can be easily and cheaply distributed wherever mail is delivered. They do not demand literacy in any language and are highly flexible – they can be consumed in many social circumstances and locations. At the same time, to the extent that pornographic photographs, as representation, have certain qualities in common with porn in other visual media, many of the arguments relating to this medium are applicable also to other forms of visual pornography.

One of the defining features of photography as against certain other forms of visual representation – painting and drawing, say – is its capacity to appear 'truthful'. Photography seems to record, rather than interpret, the piece of the world in front of the camera. A human artist may filter the 'real world' through her or his creative imagination, but the camera and lens are often regarded simply as pieces of machinery which allow an image, a duplicate, of the world to be transferred onto film. A photograph stands as evidence that whatever is inside the frame of the image 'really' happened, was 'really' there: it is authentic, convincing, true.[2] But photography actually involves just as much artifice as does any other mode of visual representation. There is plenty of scope for human intervention at every stage of making photographs: photos are no more innocent of cultural formation than any other product of human society. Nevertheless, photos do offer themselves up as in some sense real, embodying a particular kind of truth: even if they do not produce their meanings in a direct, unmediated way they often seem to do so. Photographs say to the spectator: this is actual, this is how it is, you need make no effort to understand this, you have only to recognise it – isn't this just the way you see it out there in the world?

Some types of photography, though, say so more loudly than others. At one extreme, news photography and social realist photography are boldest in their claim to tell it like it is. On the other hand, art photographs, photos bearing the signature of an 'artist of the camera', freely admit there has been creative intervention on the part of the artist-photographer, so that claims to authenticity in relation to a 'real world' become attenuated, perhaps even irrelevant. Art photography, though, is relatively insignificant in terms of most people's everyday experience of photographs. In general, photographs connote truth and authenticity when what is 'seen' by the camera eye appears to be an adequate stand-in for what is seen by the human eye. Photographs are coded, but usually so as to appear uncoded. The truth/authenticity potential of photography is tied in with the idea that seeing is believing. Photography draws on an ideology of the visible as evidence. The eye of the camera is neutral, it sees the world as it is: we look at a photograph and see a slice of the world. To complete the circuit of recording, visibility and truth set up by the photograph, there has to be someone looking at it. The spectator looks at the photograph, and the look of the camera is completed by the look of the spectator: the photograph says that these two looks are one and the same. Meaning is produced, finally, in the spectator's look: looking is crucial in reading photographs.

The spectator's look at a photograph is not limited in time, however: she or he may merely glance at the image, may study it at length, or come back to it again and again. This sets the still photo apart from other media – such as film and television – which draw on, but are not exhausted by, conventions of photographic representation. At the same time it is not usual, either, to look at a photographic still in isolation: it may be in a magazine, captioned or surrounded by print, or it may be one of a series of images to be read in sequence as a story in photos. The immediate context in which an image appears will set limits on the ways in which it is likely to be read.[3]

The spectator's look, then, is key in the reading of photographs. This look distinguishes photos from non-visual forms of representation, and also from non-photographic visual representations. Moreover, it is inflected in specific ways in relation to photographic stills as against, say, movies. The spectator can choose to gaze at length, to return again and again, to a favourite photograph. Looking may turn into contemplation, even into voyeurism. The voyeur's pleasure depends on the object of this look being unable to see him: to this extent, it is a pleasure of power, and the look a controlling one. Photographs are well equipped to produce this kind of pleasure: the apparent authenticity of what is in the image combines with the fact that it is of course actually not there – and so can be looked at for as long as desired, because the circuit of pleasure will never be broken by a returned look. Authenticity, visibility, looking, voyeurism, pleasure – these are the terms through which photographs produce meanings for their spectators. But how does all this tie in with pornography's ideological project of constructing sexual difference by, in, representation? How is this project realised in pornographic photographs?

Any sustained examination of photographic pornography will show that it draws consistently on a circumscribed set of conventions of photographic representation. These conventions relate both to the formal organisation of the pictures and also to the kinds of contents and narrative themes that repeatedly come up in them. They do, however, vary somewhat between different pornographic genres: while softcore, for example, consistently uses images of women on their own, in most forms of hardcore women are not portrayed on their own and are usually less central to what is represented. In some instances – notably gay male porn – women do not appear at all. But pornography's ideological project of constructing sexual difference usually, though by no means inevitably, demands that women be represented in some way or other. How does this work in particular images, in different types of pornographic photography?

Caught unawares

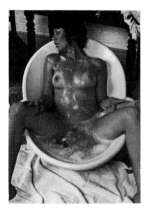

The woman in this photograph appears to have been caught by the camera in a moment of autoeroticism. She is enjoying her own body – the silky feel of underclothes on the skin, her own touch, her image in a mirror, some erotic fantasy. Alone, she is transported by her pleasure. This kind of image is one of the two staples of softcore pornography, and of all the conventions of photographic porn is the one most firmly tied to woman-as-representation: men are rarely, if ever, represented in this way. This is a quite socially acceptable, even a respectable, way of portraying women, and is often not considered pornographic at all. Well-known photographers will sign their names to images of this kind, so transforming them from cheesecake into high art. David Hamilton's series of photographs *Dreams of Young Girls*,[4] for instance, does exactly this: these images are often to be found on sale at the upmarket bookstalls of art galleries.

Her eyes are closed, she faces away from camera, but her body is wide open. The photograph pretends to be a candid shot, pretends she is unaware that the camera is there. An attractive woman takes a solitary bath and is carried away by the sensuousness of it all. The spectator sneaks a look at her enjoyment of an apparently unselfconscious moment of pleasure in herself: the Peeping Tom's favourite fantasy. Since she does not know he is there, he can take a good look at what a woman gets up to when she is on her own. He might even find out what women are really like, what their pleasure really is.

The voyeur's conviction is that the riddle of femininity will ultimately yield its solution if he looks long enough and hard enough. Since his desire is pinned to the actual process of investigation/scrutiny, though, the maintenance of desire depends upon the riddle's solution remaining just out of sight. Fortunately, the picture obliges. As a photograph, it starts out by exploiting the codes of authenticity attaching to the medium: the photo says that this woman, and so perhaps all women, do really pleasure themselves in this way. The spectator can indulge in the 'lawless seeing' permitted by the photo's reassurance that the woman is unaware of his look: her eyes are closed, her face averted. He can gaze as long as he likes at her body, with its signs of difference on display. In this photograph, though, he is denied a look at the ultimate mark of difference, her sex. But the fact that it is concealed by the bathwater only adds to the lure of investigation. This photograph is one of a sequence which tells a commonplace little story of a woman undressing: sure enough, later in the sequence the mystery of what is hidden under the bathwater is indeed revealed.

At the same time, of course, the spectator is aware that he is looking not at life but at a photograph. At a certain point, the artifice of the representation reasserts itself. On one level, this adds to his pleasure. The disposition of the woman's face suggests that she is unaware of the spectator's presence: she does not look out at him, at the camera. This is reinforced by the spectator's knowledge that this is 'only' a photograph: she could never look back at him in any case, precisely because this is nothing but a picture. A photograph, however much it may pretend to authenticity, must always in the final instance admit that this is not real, in the sense that what is in the picture is not here, but elsewhere. This very quality of absence may augment the voyeuristic pleasure of the spectator's look. On another level, though, the artifice of the photograph will ensure that his desire remains ungratified. Since he knows it is artifice, how can he be sure after all that it really is telling him anything about femininity, about woman's pleasure? The question remains unanswered: he is condemned to endless investigation.

This kind of engagement depends upon the spectator's seeing the woman in the picture as other, as a fit object of investigation-by-scrutiny. To this extent, it is a masculine engagement – which is why I have used the pronoun 'he' when discussing the spectator. The photograph speaks to a masculine subject, constructing woman as object, femininity as otherness. This does not mean that female spectators cannot, or do not, engage in a 'masculine' way with photographs like this, nor does it mean that women cannot adopt a position of voyeurism. Masculinity is not the same as maleness, even if it may be conventional in our society to construct it so. Women can and do derive pleasure from images of women, a fact which betokens the unfixity of sexual identity and the fluidity of our engagement with certain types of image. If women enjoy this picture, it is possible that they are adopting a masculine subject position in doing so. There is another possibility, however. A spectator (male or female) has the option of identifying with, rather than objectifying, the woman in the picture. The photo might evoke memories or fantasies of similar pleasures enjoyed by the spectator. In this case, the pleasure of looking is not completely voyeuristic. Indeed, an important attribute of this kind of softcore image is its openness: it may be read in a variety of ways. Its original context (a series of narratively-organised still photographs published in a men's pinup magazine) certainly proposes a masculine subject position for a male spectator. But other positions are possible, too.

In softcore pornography, the woman is usually on her own. The relationship between her and the spectator is private, one-to-one. If the photo says that the solitary woman is caught up in her own pleasure, it also puts that pleasure on display for the benefit of the spectator. She is caught unawares – but is there just for him, all the same. The image suggests that if the object of his look does not know he is there, he might discover something about her that would not otherwise be revealed – in this case, something about her sexuality, her pleasure. All the more so, perhaps, if he can sneak a look at two women enjoying each other sexually. What do women get up to when they are alone together? Lesbian scenes are a staple of the kind of pornography that bridges softcore and hardcore. Such scenes deploy some of the conventions of the stolen look at a woman alone, caught up in her own pleasure, while at the same time constructing codes for the representation, within a certain context, of more sociable sex. Lesbian scenes also neatly sidestep a cultural embargo on representing male genitalia.

Typical of this subgenre of pornography are photographs regularly published in 'adult' magazines of the sort available in many newsagents as well as in more specialised establishments. The pictures are commonly organised, without captions, in sequences readable as narratives. In one typical sequence, the first image shows two women in scanty and frilly underwear (which in all types and degrees of pornography functions as a cultural marker of femininity-as-sexuality) embrace. As the story proceeds, there is increasing emphasis on oral sex between the women, and it soon becomes clear that the objective of this story-in-pictures is to get as close a view of the action as possible: the action being what takes place around the bodily mark of woman's difference, her sex. The visible is all.

Images like this address the spectator in two distinct ways. They start by evoking voyeuristic pleasure – looking without the look being returned. The spectator can safely enjoy the fantasy that this is the kind of thing that might really go on were he not there. At the same time, though, the bodies and parts of bodies in the pictures are obligingly composed so that the spectator can get a good look at what pornography says are the really important things. The images combine an assertion of authenticity (a stolen look at a private activity) with an admission of performance, even of exhibitionism. The spectator has it both ways: he begins his investigation of femininity by looking for clues about what women do together when men are not around. The image, soliciting his gaze, draws him into what is happening, a position confirmed by revelations of 'the action' which set themselves up as authentic while at the same time operating as a display directed precisely at him. The women *are* doing it all for him, after all.

In their usual contexts, lesbian porn photos like these function not so much to celebrate women's mutual pleasure as to place it on display for a masculine spectator. Woman's pleasure is set up as an object of curiosity, which demands investigation simply because it is other. The spectator's gaze is masculine, and the image addresses him as part of the action, constructing his sexuality as masculine. The spectator, constructed as masculine, may then fantasise a leading role for himself in a little scenario *à trois*. Pornography of this kind is not intended for women – though a reading 'against the grain' is undeniably possible. Apart from the fact that, in textual terms, it speaks to a masculine spectator, it is published in magazines aimed exclusively at male consumers.

For a regime of representation that constantly proclaims itself on the side of sexual liberation, pornography hedges itself about with an extraordinary array of limits. At present, for example, it draws very firm lines around representations of male sexuality and heterosexual activity. While censorship of representations of sexual activities conventionally regarded as socially unacceptable is perhaps to be expected, it appears hard to fathom why it is that both the sexual subjectivity which sets itself up as the cultural norm (masculinity) and the sexual practice we are all meant to strive for (heterosexuality) are both in certain respects unrepresentable. Photographs of erect penises, for example, are usually confined to hardcore and to gay male pornography, while representations of acts of heterosexual intercourse are also limited in availability. Such censorships, however, far from marginalising certain sexual practices, precisely construct them as the really important ones. The paradox of the unrepresentability of heterosexual intercourse turns out to be no paradox at all: the embargo confirms the cultural ascendancy of heterosexuality and the primacy within heterosexual sex of the act of coition, the reduction within ideology of all sexual activity to conjunction of penis and vagina.

The most widely-available varieties of porn are preoccupied much more with the female than with the male body. Even in the relatively explicit 'adult' magazines, men rarely figure in photographs. When they do they never, it seems, have erections. To this extent, if pornography says that male and female are mutually exclusive categories, and that the difference between them is basically what sexuality and sexual pleasure are all about, then its examination of that pleasure is clearly rather one-sided. Woman is subjected to a much more thoroughgoing investigation-by-scrutiny than man. The spectator is addressed as if the quest for knowledge, pleasure, closure, were directed exclusively towards woman and the feminine. He can find out a lot more about the woman's body – what it looks like, at least, for in pornography seeing is all – than about the man's. The feminine is constructed as the principal object of enquiry because the masculine is taken for granted as the place from which the spectator looks.

Photographs which show acts of coition are nevertheless available to those prepared to take the trouble to seek them out. In Britain, they are confined mainly to imported pornography, Scandinavian hardcore in particular. Such material deals in representations which are subject to certain kinds of censorship, and importers run the risk of having their merchandise seized by Customs: there is more than a tinge of illicitness about the whole business, therefore. Moreover, pornography of this type is retailed only in specialist establishments, and it calls for a certain amount of motivation and effort, not to mention cash, to obtain it. All this doubtless fuels the consumer's conviction that something really worth knowing about is likely to be revealed.

Such pornography has a number of preoccupations. First of all, it draws on the notion – a feature also of less 'explicit' porn – that male–female differences are reducible to bodily parts which are exclusively sexual in function. More specifically, however, it insists that the joining of these disparate parts is the moment when sexual difference is ultimately confirmed. Finally, in some types of hardcore, attempts are made to represent orgasm visually, to present it as the culminating moment of sex, the Big O, the gratifying resolution of a narrative of sexual activity. One might perhaps imagine that orgasm does not lend itself very easily to photographic representation: but pornography has ways of getting around this problem, usually by privileging the male orgasm over the female and equating it with ejaculation.

Because of its deployment of certain conventions of photographic representation, and even more perhaps because of the atmosphere of illicitness and censorship surrounding its consumption, pornography of this kind can be particularly forceful in what it says. It insists that the moment of penetration in male–female intercourse is what sex is fundamentally about, and that the goal is orgasm (read male ejaculation). This revelation carries all the power of recondite knowledge. The voyeuristic pleasure evoked by catching people in the act, however, may also acquire some of the more disturbing resonances of the primal scene, when the infant is witness to its parents' sexual activity. To this extent, certain kinds of pornography may combine pleasure and unease – perhaps even at moments threatening to disrupt, rather than confirm, the spectator's masculinity.

Bits and pieces

Psychoanalytic accounts of the construction of sexuality and the production of the Unconscious point to the formative quality of certain moments in the infant's relationships with those to whom it is closest – in our society, usually members of its immediate family. These moments carry all the power of intense melodrama. The Oedipus complex is charged with the erotic and jealous drama of the eternal triangle, the primal scene with the horror of an awful truth and the trauma of coming to terms with it. Psychoanalysis, like pornography, is obsessed with bodily differences, and the most elemental of the scenarios enacted in its family melodrama are pivoted around exactly such differences. Is it perhaps part of pornography's project, then, to replay these elemental scenarios, to participate in the psychic relations through which we are constructed as sexual subjects?

It is significant that classic psychoanalytic accounts of these processes are just as one-sided as pornography itself: psychoanalysis speaks almost exclusively, and certainly with the greatest conviction, of the preoccupations of the infant male, of the development of a masculine sexuality. The little boy realises that his mother has no penis, that she may be different from him. He catches a glimpse of his parents in an act which is intimate, but seems also to be violent. He is excluded: he is not, after all, the centre of the Universe. Nothing is secure anymore. How will he be able to continue enjoying the pleasure he gets from his own body? Will he lose his mother's love? Does his father's love matter to him, or is father's power in a patriarchal society more desirable than mother's love? Each of these moments is associated, in psychoanalytic accounts, with looking and seeing: the infant sees his mother's genitals, steals a look at his parents copulating. And certain aspects of what he sees stand out in his memory because they are so important to him: they are recalled as it were in close-up.[5]

These psychic processes are echoed in a particular convention of photographic pornography, namely the fragmentation, within the image, of the human body. In pornography, photographs are often composed in such a way that a particular bodily part is greatly emphasised. Or it may even fill the whole of the picture, in which case the body is fragmented, cut up, by the frame. In our society, only one convention of partial framing in visual images is generally regarded as an adequate substitute of bodily part for whole: this is the portrait. In the portrait, attention is directed at the subject's face. The face stands in for the person's whole being: the subject's essential humanity is seen as inhabiting his or her face, the 'window of the soul'. Within this perspective, an abstracted bodily part other than the face may be regarded as an expropriation of the subject's individuality. In consequence, the tendency of some pornographic photographs to isolate bits of bodies may be read as a gesture of dehumanisation.

But porn's attention to bits of bodies is never random. Pornography is preoccupied with what it regards as the signifiers of sexual difference and sexuality: genitals, breasts, buttocks. To the extent that pornography circulates such images, it also constructs human beings as sexual bodies. However, the process of fragmentation is by no means disinterested as regards gender. Although it is not difficult to find examples of fetishised representations of the male body, it is much more often the female body and its representation which receives this kind of treatment. Mass-circulation 'girlie' magazines routinely go in for mild forms of fetishisation, with their emphasis on women's breasts and buttocks, while many of the more explicit, but still widely-circulated, 'adult' magazines go a good deal further, in particular with close-ups of female genitals. Taken together, the girlie magazine and the newsstand adult magazine markets undoubtedly account for the bulk of pornography use. These forms of pornography demonstrate quite clearly the processes by which woman in particular is sexualised within representation.

Pinup photography seldom actually fragments the body, however. The subject's face is invariably included in the image, perhaps because facial expression provides some possibility of fixing meaning, of guiding the spectator's reading, in representations which may often be open to a range of interpretations. It is common, too, in the pinup for most or all of the subject's body to be included in the picture. Such images are nevertheless preoccupied with a limited number of parts of the female body: the interest is relatively diffuse, however, and always contexted – in the sense that even if only one or two body parts are emphasised, they are always shown as belonging to a 'whole' woman. Pinup and softcore photography's interest in the female body is confined to a small repertoire of parts – those which mark the woman as feminine, not-male, different. This preoccupation is evident not only in the way particular images are composed – lighting, accessories, posture, gesture, framing – but also by virtue of the very repetitiveness of certain poses across a range of photos: the bosom thrust forward, the raised buttocks and, in recent years, the open legs and crotch shot. Softcore draws on and transforms conventions through which the female nude is represented in high art, placing them within a mass-market context.[6] There is a circumscribed, almost a rigid, set of codes or conventions of representation of the body in this type of photography, conventions with which even the most naive spectator is likely to be familiar.

For example, the woman's body is angled towards the camera to offer maximum display of whatever part of the body is at the moment being emphasised; breasts are accentuated by the placement of arms and elbows in certain ways, and so on. These poses are so commonplace – pinups of this kind appear every day in some popular newspapers[7] – that their cultural meanings acquire a degree of naturalisation. The woman in the picture, and so perhaps woman in general, is constructed as interesting because of her body, or certain parts of it. The photograph says: look at this, this body is there for you to look at, and you will enjoy looking at it. The formal arrangement of the body, the way it is displayed, solicits the spectator's gaze. The conventions of pinup photography work to construct the body, usually the female body, as a spectacle: and the female body is a spectacle because parts of it – the parts that say 'this is a woman' – are pleasurable to look at.

The project of the softcore female pinup is to construct sexual difference in representation by defining it in terms of, even reducing it to, bodily parts marked culturally, and/or within the context of the image, as feminine. Their conviction is that sexuality equals femininity: their promise that femininity may be investigated, even understood, by scrutinising its visible marks.

With the move away from pinups and softcore towards hardcore pornography, the fetishisation of body parts by their accentuation within the image gives way to a more literal fragmentation. The spectator's attention is directed to certain parts of the body in isolation, and interest is likely to be centred more exclusively on genitals as signifiers of sexual difference. In softcore, particularly when it appears in glossy magazines, representations of the female body are often motivated (or justified) in terms of notions of 'glamour' or 'art'. In these magazines, images are also commonly accorded some degree of narrative motivation: the spectator is given a set of pictures which include various conventional pinup poses, but which also tell a little story – a woman undresses and takes a bath, a woman undresses and stands next to a window where she can be seen from outside, and so on. The images are arranged in sequence according to what is revealed of her body. The culmination of the series is currently, in the most 'explicit' pinup photography, the 'split beaver', in which the signifier of the woman's difference is fully displayed, but always with her entire body in frame. Art, glamour, narrativity – terms which strain to keep pinup photography on the side of respectability.

With hardcore, all such pretence is dropped, and the spectator's obsession frankly acknowledged. A particularly common theme in pornographic photographs picks up on the desire – constrained in the pinup by self-censorship as well as by its own formal conventions – to focus upon the woman's sex as the fundamental sign of her otherness. Pornography which operates outside the constraints attendant on the pinup can get down to business right away, and show female genitals in full close-up. The woman in the picture, says this type of pornography, is anonymous: or rather her identity resides in her sex – not in her clothes, nor in her face, nor indeed in any other part of her body. The vagina in the picture stands in for the enigma of the feminine. The full-page, full-colour close-up invites the spectator to enter into the mystery, suggests that something crucial is to be learned from his contemplation of it. If photographic images assume that what cannot be looked at is of no consequence, then they also propose that nothing outside the frame is of any significance.

Fragmentation is much more common in photographic images of the female body than of the male: in pornography, it is the woman's sex that is constructed as the prime object of the spectator's curiosity. The image addresses the spectator as desiring – desiring specifically to penetrate this mystery, to come to terms with it, to know it – and says that knowledge is to be secured through looking. If the desire to understand implies that the spectator is in some sense set apart from the object of his look, then the pornographic image constructs the woman's sex as other, as *object* of a masculine gaze. The object of enquiry is objectified. Pornography conflates femininity with femaleness, femaleness with female sexuality, and female sexuality with a particular part of the female anatomy. At the same time, it attempts to render these qualities visible, and thus fit objects of observation. The subject–object split proposed by positivist science puts in an unexpected appearance in pornography, then: porn places the masculine on the side of the subject, the feminine on the side of the object, of enquiry. Although it can be argued that in some degree all pornography does this, pornography which preoccupies itself specifically with female genitals *in abstracto* demonstrates with particular clarity the peculiar combination of observation and objectification that characterises the pornographic as a mode of address.

The invitation

Pornographic images participate in photography's more general project of privileging the visible, of equating visibility with truth. But porn inflects this concern with its own ruling obsessions – sexuality and sexual difference – which are made visible, become a spectacle which reveals itself to the spectator. The spectator is invited to look – with the promise that he will derive both pleasure and knowledge from his looking. His quest is mapped out for him in pornographic photographs – which always speak to his desire for pleasurable looking.

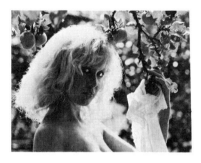

The desire for pleasurable looking – scopophilia – manifests itself in a variety of ways, voyeurism being only one. In voyeurism, the subject of the look, the Peeping Tom, separates himself in the act of looking from the object, which cannot look back at him. But although the power inherent in the voyeur's look, the power of catching its object unawares, may be pleasurable in itself, the object's unfathomable desire remains. What if she is not interested in him after all? Pornography promises to circumvent such a threat to the voyeur's pleasure by saying he can have it both ways. While in various respects the photograph proposes that the woman in the picture is unaware of the spectator's look, the risk of her indifference is mitigated by the fact that her body may at the same time be arranged as if on display for him. This implies an unspoken exhibitionism on the part of the object of the look, thus permitting the spectator a twofold pleasure. This combination of visual pleasures is taken one step further in what is probably the most commonplace of all the conventions of pornography, of softcore in particular, the 'come-on'.

The woman in the picture above, far from being caught unawares in her own pleasure, now seems openly to acknowledge the spectator by her direct look at the camera. This is a particular kind of look – the head is tilted so that her glance is slightly angled rather than face-on. The indirect

41

look signifies sexual invitation or teasing, a reading underscored by the cultural connotations of the slightly parted
lips. This facial expression, particularly in combination with
the conventionalised display of the rest of the woman's
body, may be read as an invitation. The spectator is lured by
the picture's assurance that he is the one the woman wants,
him and no-one else. On the level at which the photograph
promises authenticity, exhibitionism wins out over voyeurism: the 'come-on' look suggests that the woman is
purposefully displaying her body for the spectator, that she
knows he is there and is inviting him quite openly to take a
good look.

At the same time, though, because this is after all 'only' a
photograph, not a real woman, an element of voyeurism
persists, because she is of course not 'really' looking at him.
The spectator's fantasy is given free rein: in one sense, there
is no risk of disappointment – he is quite safe because it is
only a picture and the woman in it will never, in real life,
turn him down or make demands which he cannot satisfy.
By the same token, of course, he can never 'really' possess
her. But the come-on in the photograph works – and to
judge by the frequency with which we see it, keeps on
working – precisely because it is such a tease. Desire is
fuelled because in the final instance its object is unattainable
– and unthreatening.

The come-on is perhaps the more culturally prominent of
the two staples of softcore pornography (the other being the
image of the solitary woman caught up in her own
pleasure). In both, though, facial expression functions
crucially to produce meaning: if the one – the come-on –
offers a direct sexual invitation, the other puts woman's
autonomous sexual pleasure on display for the spectator. In
pinup photos, the face is a key signifier, a central element in
the image's production of meaning and its address to the
spectator. It is never left out of the picture, for pinups
cannot be as specific, nor as explicit, as hardcore in their
reduction of sexual difference to bodily difference. Pinups,
in consequence, are more open, capable of a wider range of
readings, than hardcore. In a relatively open image, the

fixation of meaning depends partly on the extent to which textual signifiers operate in accord with one another. It also depends in some degree on what the spectator brings to his reading of the image. In the instance of pinup photographs, the formal organisation of the images themselves, taken together with the contexts in which they normally appear (men's 'entertainment' magazines), would as a rule privilege a 'masculine' reading by male consumers. Their potential for instability, though, does suggest that pinup photographs may be open to a range of readings, particularly when placed in different contexts.

Facial expression, the come-on look in particular, is a key moment in the pinup's construction of a masculine subject position for the spectator. In offering itself as both spectacle and truth, the photograph suggests that the woman in the picture, rather than the image itself, is responsible for soliciting the spectator's gaze. In doing this, the photograph constructs her body as an object of scrutiny, suggesting at the same time that female sexuality is active, that women may invite sex. The pinup's singular preoccupation with the female body is tied in with the project of defining the 'true' nature of female sexuality. Femaleness and femininity are constructed as a set of bodily attributes reducible to a sexuality which puts itself on display for a masculine spectator. In these ways the pinup invites the spectator to participate in a masculine definition of femininity.

Identifying power

Pornographic photographs engage the spectator's scopophilia, promise him pleasure in looking. Because of the definitive absence of what is represented in the photographs, there is always an element of voyeuristic pleasure in the spectator's looking. This is true even when photography's tendency to proclaim authenticity on its own behalf adds to voyeurism visual pleasures of other kinds. The conventionalised display of bodies to the spectator, the fetishising of certain bodily attributes, the come-on look, all give pornography an exhibitionistic quality, offering the spectator relief from guilt about his voyeurism. Voyeurism, and voyeurism-plus-exhibitionism, are relations of looking which separate the source of the look from its object. While |luring the spectator with the promise of visual pleasure,) pornography in the final instance excludes him from the action. (Frustrating though this may be on one level, on another a lack of closure opens up a space for the spectator's fantasy, a space where he is free to complete the action as he pleases, in his own imagination.\

The spectator's exclusion, however, may at times be mitigated by an address which permits, even requires, him to identify with individuals in the picture. Characteristic of many forms of narrative is the reader's identification with a character in the fiction, or at least an interest in what will befall him or her. This interest keeps the reader involved throughout the story. The reader's desire is for some satisfactory outcome for the character with whom he or she identifies. If all photographic pornography evokes voyeurism, some types may also solicit a degree of identification on the spectator's part. This is particularly the case where pictures are organised as narratives in which the same characters appear throughout.

However, in pornographic stories, literary as well as visual, characters are never very strongly developed as psychologically rounded human beings. They perform functions, they take on roles already fixed within the commonplace fantasies that porn constructs – the sexually active woman, the Peeping Tom, the plumber out on his rounds. In porn, characters *are* what they do, and given a minimal amount of familiarity with the genre, the reader needs little by way of explanation in order to understand what is going on. In this sense, pornographic stories are often quite economical, even if rarely rated for their artistic value (but porn's business is after all not to please the critics). Pornography has a good deal in common with other simple forms of narrative, stories in which characters are no more than what they do and the reader has some general idea, as soon as the story begins, of who is going to do what to whom, and with what outcome. In a fairy tale, for instance, we know the woodcutter is the hero who will in the end win the hand of the princess. Our interest is in what he has to go through in order to reach his goal. In many respects, pornographic stories work like fairy tales.

Pornographic narratives have a stock cast of characters, and the acculturated reader already knows the sorts of things they are likely to get up to. Porn's task is to put these activities into words or pictures, to provide characters with every possible narrative opportunity to perform their sexual exploits.[8] Photographic pornography which invites the spectator's identification along with his voyeurism is most often in the hardcore category. These stories-in-pictures set up a limited and familiar range of character types and scenarios – a handyman calls on a housewife who answers the door in her negligée, a hitchhiker is picked up by a truck driver, a man passing a house sees a woman sunbathing nude in her garden. The outcome of the story the spectator already knows, but his desire is of course to *see* it. Once the scene is set, pornography can get down to the real action.

In general, the harder the porn, the more people, and – significantly – the more men in it. The tendency for men to feature more often in hardcore than in softcore pornography may be explained to some extent in terms of the relatively strong cultural taboo on representations of male sexual organs and of sexual activities involving men – though this of course begs the question of why the taboo exists in the first place. However, the presence of men also allows for a new variant of address 'in the masculine': the male spectator may identify with a male protagonist. Although he is obviously not obliged to do so, pornography may nevertheless invite such an identification in various ways.

If men's participation as protagonists in the action becomes significant in hardcore pornography in general, the invitation to the spectator to identify is particularly strong in particular subgenres of hardcore. As voyeurism gives way to identification, the spectator sheds much of the responsibility for producing his own sexual fantasy, if only because the fantasy is more likely to be actually there in the picture. If hardcore porn is quite specific in its representation of sexual activities, it constructs a relatively limited range of possibilities for sexual fantasy. Identification may be said to go hand-in-hand with closure, with fixation of meaning. In instances where pornography evokes hostile and aggressive aspects of sexuality, the spectator may welcome the relief from guilt offered by identification and closure.

Sadomasochistic pornography – especially of the kind which details violence done to women by men – has been the subject of a good deal of concern of late, not only because for many women it is so disturbing in itself, but also because – or so it has been argued – more of it is being produced now than ever before.[9] Because of its capacity to disgust, it may be difficult for anyone who does not share the fantasies constructed by sexually violent pornography even to begin to understand the nature of the pleasure it gives to those who do enjoy it.[10] However, consumers who bring to their reading of this pornography a preoccupation with domination and sexuality-as-power may construct their pleasure around identification with its protagonists. Sadomasochistic pornography re-enacts a master–slave scenario of sex-as-power: so that, for example, where women are subjected to sexual violence, mastery is constructed as operating on the side of the masculine. To this extent, it participates in pornography's more routine insistence on sexual difference, except that in this case sexual difference is reduced to relations of power rather than, or as well as, to bodily attributes.

But as with more commonplace variants of pornography, here too the female body frequently becomes the object of scrutiny and investigation: though not in this case as a relation between spectator and image, but within the image and the story themselves. This betokens an obsession with the otherness of femininity, which in common with many forms of otherness seems to contain a threat to the onlooker. Curiosity turns to terror, investigation to torture, the final affirmation of the objecthood of the other. The feminine here represents a threat to the masculine, a threat which demands containment. Sexually violent pornography of this kind concretises this wish for containment in representations which address the spectator as masculine, and place the masculine on the side of container of the threat. It insists that sexuality and power are inseparable.

3

Sexual disguise and cinema

Rep dependent
on existing
Circulation of constructed
Categories

Pornographic photographs are not alone in their preoccupation with sexual difference: other visual representations are also interested, in their own ways, in this question. Sexual difference is dealt with in a variety of ways across different media, genres and forms, is produced through diverse codes and conventions. All representations are coded: they do not merely reflect a world outside the bounds of the text, but mediate external discourses, as it were rewriting and reconstructing them. Representations – or readings available from them – are constituted by a series of discourses which circulate both within and beyond the text itself. Thus, for instance, the appeal pornography makes to distinctions between masculinity and femininity refers outwards to constructions of these categories already in cultural circulation, drawing on and reproducing them in its own forms of address.

What happens, though, when the masculine–feminine dualism becomes so prominent an issue that the very cultural stability proposed by the categories is rendered subject to challenge? This chapter looks at cinema, and specifically at some 'mainstream' films, in which, as a central element of plot, characters assume the conventional clothing of the opposite sex, and a confusion of gender categories ensues. It was written as a result of an invitation to give a talk at a weekend event of screenings and discussions around the topic of crossdressing and cinema. Because this was not an area I had worked on before, the first thing I did in preparing the talk was to search the literature for relevant material. To my surprise, there was extraordinarily little. True, there were a number of interesting review-type articles, mostly in the gay press, on individual films, but none of these had any analytical pretensions. At a general level, the question seems hardly to have been approached at all within film studies – though it has, to a certain extent, been addressed in literary theory. It is interesting to speculate why it is that, despite the lasting popularity of a number of crossdressing films, the question of sexual disguise and cinema should remain more-or-less neglected by film theorists. Perhaps, *pace* the critical derision and theoretical neglect suffered until quite recently by the 'woman's weepie', crossdressing films have not been considered worthy of serious attention precisely because of their popularity and their particular appeal to a despised section of the population?

Be that as it may, in attempting to produce some sort of analysis of films with which I – in common with everyone else, it seems – had only the most naive acquaintance, I fell back on familiar strategies: I thought about codes of narrative cinema and how the theme of sexual disguise is articulated by them. In the quest to understand how crossdressing films work, this turned out to be productive, but not entirely satisfactory. Taking account of the cultural meanings which surround crossdressing as a social practice, however, did seem to add usefully to the broadly semiotic approach I started out with. On a cultural level, crossdressing may be understood as a mode of performance in which – through play on a disjunction between clothes and body – the socially constructed nature of sexual difference is foregrounded and even subjected to comment: what appears natural, then, reveals itself as artifice.

In dominant cinema, stories are told through the medium of the moving picture according to a circumscribed set of conventions. Films consequently produce meanings in ways different from, say, still photographs. In films of sexual

49

disguise, cinematic conventions – notably codes of narrativity, genre and spectacle – intersect cultural meanings surrounding practices of crossdressing. This chapter attempts to trace the operation of various textual and cultural codes in specific crossdressing films.

Analysing films in this way, unpacking the various layers of meaning at work in them, demands in this instance attention to the particular ways in which sexual difference is constructed. In films of the kind considered here, stories pivot around mistaken identifications of gender. The narrativisation of such themes may provoke questions about the ways in which gender is socially constructed: it may even subject to a certain interrogation the culturally taken-for-granted dualities of male/female and masculine/feminine. Just how transgressive such a strategy can finally be when deployed through the conventions of dominant cinema is arguable. But perhaps the pleasure of the most popular films of sexual disguise does nevertheless lie in their capacity to offer, at least momentarily, a vision of fluidity of gender options; to provide a glimpse of 'a world outside the order normally seen or thought about' – a utopian prospect of release from the ties of sexual difference that bind us into meaning, discourse, culture.

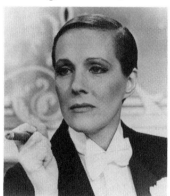

Victor/Victoria

How many films have been made in which characters take on the conventional clothing of the opposite sex? Even restricting the list to mainstream film, there appears to be quite a lot of cinematic crossdressing about: *Queen Christina, Some Like It Hot, Psycho, Tootsie, Privates on Parade, Sylvia Scarlett, Thunderbolt and Lightfoot, Dressed to Kill, Calamity Jane, Victor/Victoria*. . . .

But why crossdressing? How does it work in these very different films? A move away from listing titles towards analysing film texts provokes interesting questions, not all of them to do directly with cinema. What cultural meanings are drawn on and constructed in representations of crossdressing? How are such meanings worked over, transformed and recirculated as they intersect pre-existing forms, discourses, genres and modes of representation? Looked at in this light, the subject of crossdressing and cinema assumes its place within the wider arena of cultural production. And yet, of course, cinema has its own specificity as a mode of representation, its own apparatus of institutional contexts, genres and modes of address, within which meanings of any sort – including meanings surrounding crossdressing – are produced in particular ways. This localised work of meaning-making does nevertheless take place within the wider social/cultural contexts in which crossdressing assumes and organises certain meanings: and approaching the question of how cinema activates these meanings in its own way calls for a negotiation of broader issues.

This essay considers first of all how crossdressing, or rather representations of crossdressing, draw upon and rework certain sets of cultural meanings and ideologies. It then addresses the issue of crossdressing in narrative representations: how crossdressing as a fictional moment organises stories of various kinds, particularly in films. Finally, cinematic representation is dealt with in its specificity as it intersects crossdressing as a set of cultural meanings organised narratively. The significance of – and hopefully the justification for – this holding back on the specifically cinematic should become apparent when the question of precisely what it means to look at a film is considered.[1]

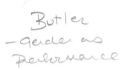

Crossdressing, performance and sexual difference

As a set of cultural meanings, crossdressing intersects two discourses. It draws on meanings centring on the one hand on performance, and on the other on constructs of gender identity and sexual difference. Understood in its everyday sense, performance is allied with acting, and acting is regarded as an activity that involves pretence, dissimulation, an intent to seem to be something or someone one is, in reality, not. An actor's role is assumed like a mask, the mask concealing the performer's 'true self'. The disguise is a cover, and in many schools of acting the more the audience is taken in by the performance, the better that performance is judged to be. In effecting a distance between assumed persona and real self, the practice of performance constructs a subject which is both fixed in the distinction between role and self and at the same time, paradoxically, called into question in the very act of performance. For over against the 'real self', performance poses the possibility of a mutable self, of a fluidity of subjectivity.

Discourses on gender identity and sexual difference hold together a range of notions centring on biological sex, social gender, sexual identification and sexual object choice. The incorporation of these in constructs of gender identity is a historically-grounded ideological project whose effect, it has been argued, has been to set up a heterogeneous and determinate set of biological, physical, social, psychological and psychic constructs as a unitary, fixed and unproblematic attribute of human subjectivity. Within this ideological project, subjectivity is always gendered and every human being is, and remains, either male or female. From this fundamental difference flows a succession of discourses on identification and sexuality. Moreover, in ideology gender identity is not merely absolute: it also lies at the very heart of human subjectivity. Gender is what crucially defines us, so that an ungendered subject cannot, in this view, be human. The human being, in other words, is a gendered subject. And so a fixed subjectivity and a gendered subjectivity are, in ideology, one and the same.

Together, performance and gender identity incorporate a range of meanings which are activated and reconstituted in a particular way in the instance of crossdressing. Such meanings are produced across a number of different axes, often in a contradictory manner. Crossdressing, by definition, involves clothing: and in itself clothing signifies. It carries a range of meanings, the most culturally prominent of which pivot on gender. In many societies, our own included, dress is gender specific. Clothing is associated with gender, serving as an outward mark of difference, of a fundamental attribute of the wearer's identity. But so to identify dress with gender identity, and gender identity with selfhood, is to step into a minefield of contradiction. What are the implications for a subjectivity which is held to be fixed and absolute of a mark of such a subjectivity that is conventional and in consequence changeable? Far from being a fixed signifier of a fixed gender identity, clothing has the potential to disguise, to alter, even to reconstruct, the wearer's self. Clothing can dissemble – it may be costume, mask, masquerade. Put another way, clothing can embody performance. As a means to, even the substance of, a commutable persona, clothing as performance threatens to undercut the ideological fixity of the human subject.

If clothing can be costume, capable of being modified at the wearer's will, it follows that the gender identity conventionally signified by dress may be just as easily changeable. Change your clothes and change your self. Change your clothes and change your sex. The potential threat to fixed subjectivity and gender identity represented by clothing goes a long way towards explaining the social prohibitions on some kinds of crossdressing, and the containment of others within traditionally acceptable forms and practices.

In its performance aspect, clothing sets up a play between visible outward appearance – in this case, gender as signified by dress – and an essence which may not be visible but is nonetheless held to be more 'real' than appearance – here the gender of the person whose true nature may be concealed, both literally and metaphorically, beneath the clothes. What is at stake in this expression of the dualism of appearance and essence is a fundamentalism of the body, an appeal to bodily attributes as final arbiter of a basic truth. The truth lies under the clothing, and although it might well be expected that in ordinary circumstances it will not and should not do so, clothing can obscure rather than reveal the truth. Dress constantly poses the possibility of distance between body and clothing, between 'true' self, the fixed gender of ideology, and assumed persona. Crossdressing as a realisation of such a potential turns this distance to account, constructing sexual disguise as a play upon the fixity and the fluidity of gender identity.

It may be useful at this point to compare sexual disguise with dandyism, in that – although the two practices differ in their articulation of sexual difference – both foreground the performance aspect of dress, and in so doing activate a certain irony. The irony implicit in the dandy's presence may be compared with the working of the ironic figure in rhetoric, which is marked by a 'wilful alienation' – both from an accepted order or norm of speech and also as a potential effect on the onlooker.[2] In its specificity crossdressing, with its play on the distance between a gendered body and gendered clothing, also opens up a space of self-referentiality. In this sense, crossdressing comments, with irony, on the conflation in ideology of body, gender, gender identity and subjectivity. If clothing as performance threatens to undercut the subject fixed in ideology, crossdressing as a particular expression of it goes one step further. It highlights the centrality of gender constructs in processes of subjectivity and comments upon a culturally salient means by which a would-be fixed gender identity is marked and constructed. It subverts the construct, offering at the same time ironic comment on its status as convention. By calling attention to the artifice of gender identity, crossdressing effects a 'wilful alienation' from the fixity of that identity: it has the potential, in consequence, to denaturalise it, to 'make it strange'. Crossdressing, then, may denaturalise that phenomenon held in our culture to be most evidently and pre-eminently natural: sexual difference.

54

But if crossdressing is capable of denaturalising sexual difference, is this potential always realised in practice? If not, in what circumstances is it realised and in what circumstances contained? Since the present concern is with representation, such questions are most productively addressed by considering the contexts in which crossdressing is represented and by attending to crossdressing texts and how they produce meaning. A more limited consideration of crossdressing in fictional narratives demands further specification of context, and directs the manner in which questions about crossdressing and sexual difference are articulated.

Crossdressing and narrativity

Fictional narratives involving crossdressing, it may be argued, problematise the ideological construction of sexual difference as natural and absolute. In this sense, they are always *about* the fixity or otherwise of gender identity, and raise the problem more or less centrally as a narrative theme. But this is not to suggest that in such texts the ideological fixity of sexual difference is necessarily subject to challenge, for this depends on a variety of textual and contextual considerations, including the structure, trajectory and viewpoint of the narrative itself and the social and historical contexts of its production, distribution and reception. Although the main emphasis of the present argument is textual rather than contextual, its bracketing of questions of context is provisional rather than methodologically prescriptive: for textual investigation should invariably generate contextual inquiry.

In examining crossdressing in modern literary narratives and in arguing that although crossdressing in fiction may well, as metaphor, subvert sexual difference it may equally well confirm it, Sandra Gilbert has attempted to move beyond a purely formalist treatment of individual texts.[3] Subversion or confirmation of sexual difference depends, she says, on literary genre and reader–text relations, as well as on internal textual organisation. So, for example, citing

55

the Nighttown episode in James Joyce's *Ulysses*, Gilbert
argues that this 'male modernist transvestite fantasy' is
sexually compensatory, that its effect is to reinforce the fixity
of sexual difference and the social/sexual hierarchies erected
upon it. *Ulysses* is contrasted with Virginia Woolf's *Orlando*
which, in the transformations undergone through the
centuries by the novel's main character, is seen as offering a
'visionary multiplicity' of gender, an androgynous subversion
of gender fixity. These two literary examples seem to
indicate that, as far as reader–text relations are concerned,
the denaturalising potential of a crossdressing text relates
directly to its openness.

The opposition of openness and closure in literary texts
recalls Roland Barthes's distinction between the pleasure to
be obtained from the closure or resolution of the classic
narrative and the 'bliss' (*jouissance*) of the text which defies
such closure.[4] Both are clearly relations of reading: the
pleasure of the former is the satisfaction of completion, of
having all the ends tied up, while the bliss of the latter is the
unsettling, the movement of the subject produced in
reading, which goes beyond – or is outside – the pleasure of
the fixation of the subject–reader of the classic narrative. As
reader–text relations, both openness and closure – both bliss
and pleasure – may be generated across a single text.
However, as Barthes has often suggested, closure is a mark
of culturally dominant narrative forms, forms whose trajectory is always towards resolution, the closing over of gaps
that may indeed have been opened up and even looked into:
for moments of *jouissance* may erupt in texts which still
remain, in the final instance, texts of closure.

To the extent that it denaturalises sexual difference,
crossdressing threatens to disrupt an apparently natural
order. Narratives involving crossdressing – representations
concerned in one way or another with gender identity and
its mutability – always, in offering the promise of a
'visionary multiplicity' of gender relations, open up a space
for *jouissance*. But many of them, as Gilbert's comments on
Ulysses would indicate, go no further than to hint at a
possibility that is ultimately closed off in the revelation of

the body beneath the clothes. A quest to uncover the truth of the concealed body may be precisely the desire that activates a narrative of sexual disguise. When the body is confirmed as the location of an absolute difference, this desire is gratified in the pleasure offered in the resolution. If crossdressing narratives always in some measure problematise gender identity and sexual difference, then, many do so only to confirm finally the absoluteness of both, to reassert a 'natural' order of fixed gender and unitary subjectivity. Nevertheless, the denaturalising potential of sexual disguise may be carried through, in texts which construct openness throughout, which pose from beginning to end fluidity of gender, androgyny, multiplicity of identifications and subjectivity in process.

In fictions of sexual disguise, openness and closure are articulated in the first instance in the organisation of their narratives, which involve at least one character who assumes the conventional clothes of the opposite sex, or who might be suspected of not, in terms of gender, being what his or her clothing would signify. Such characters are positioned in a variety of ways in relation to events in the fiction. Their positioning varies according to the structure of the narrative – what sets the story in motion and how its resolution is brought about; the trajectory of the narrative – how events between beginning and end are constructed in relation to one another; and the point-of-view of the narrative – how the reader is placed in relation to the telling of the story and the knowledge the reader possesses, *vis-à-vis* characters in the fiction, about events.

In crossdressing narratives, sexual disguise must usually be accounted for, given some sort of explanation within the story. Where a character assumes sexual disguise during the course of the narrative, this move typically constitutes a disruption that sets the story in motion: in this case, the reader is usually aware from the outset of the character's 'true' gender. There exists in fact a set of stock narrative situations which motivate, or explain, a character's assumption of sexual disguise. In the light of some of the arguments advanced above, it is interesting to note that in a number of

narrative films involving crossdressing, performance constitutes a central theme, and characters assuming sexual
disguise are often (in the story) performers by profession. In
such a situation, sexual disguise is explained plausibly in
terms of the character's job and its requirements. When, as
is often the case, crossdressing narratives go to great lengths
outwardly to disavow any suggestion of perversion attaching
to such characters (and to the actors playing them), sexual
perversion still often works as a subtext. Indeed, a play of
acknowledgment and disavowal around sexuality and sexual
perversion can be a fertile source of comedy. In conjunction
with the performance motif, this is what identifies a certain
type of crossdressing film with the genre of musical comedy.

In films of this type, the story typically opens with the
plight of an unemployed or otherwise desperate performer
who resorts to sexual disguise in order to get work.
Beginnings of this kind characterise some of the most
celebrated crossdressing films – *Some Like It Hot* (Wilder,
1959), *Victor/Victoria* (Edwards, 1982) and *Tootsie* (Pollack,
1982), for example. Each of these has performers of some
sort – musicians, singer, actor – as central characters. Two
are musical comedies, while one – *Tootsie* – aspires to be
something of a serious treatment of an actor's persistence
and professionalism: though, characteristic of the 'performance' crossdressing film, there are also a number of highly
comic moments.

While films in which sexual disguise is explained as
performance may downplay outward connotations of sexual
perversion, other crossdressing films bring such associations
to the centre of the story. When perversity substitutes for
performance, sexual disguise becomes transvestism – a
practice constituted, in the clinical discourse which names it,
as pathological. The sexually disguised character is constructed as sick, or criminal, or both: and crossdressing, far from
being comic, becomes threatening. In crossdressing films of
this type, narratives are rarely activated by a character's
assumption of sexual disguise. A more typical opening
move is a 'villainy' such as a disappearance, a theft, or –
likeliest of all – a murder.[5] If the villain at some point in the

58

story adopts sexual disguise, the crossdressing is constructed narratively as either a symptom of his psychopathy or an outward sign of his wickedness and depravity. Crossdressing, in other words, explains why the villain does what he does: for in the world of this sort of story, personal pathology is a plausible and a sufficient explanation of criminal acts. Such inflections identify films of this kind with the genre of thriller. — *cross dresser is not villain*

Most narrative films involving sexual disguise can probably be identified as belonging to, or at least as close to, the genres either of thriller or of musical comedy. Different from one another though these may be in other respects, it is significant that in both genres crossdressing has to be accounted for in one way or another within the narrative. Explanations, furthermore, often constitute a central element of plot, sometimes even activating the narrative. In this sense, these films construct crossdressing as in varying degrees culturally 'strange'.

Within the classic narrative, intradiegetic explanations for crossdressing seem to operate both at a general level – facing outward, as it were, to the social/cultural context in which meanings attaching to crossdressing are produced, and also, more specifically, such explanations look inward to the conventions of the classic narrative and of certain film genres. In the musical comedy, sexual disguise acquires cultural plausibility by reference to such values as the work ethic and the necessity for economic survival, while in the thriller it is naturalised through discourses on sexual deviance, psychopathology and criminality. In either case, cultural references work within the respective generic conventions of the musical comedy and the thriller, at the same time reproducing and reconstructing those conventions. Intratextual reference to cultural and generic convention operates effectively to contain the denaturalising potential of crossdressing narrative. In this sense, such reference marks a pervasive closure which operates in addition to the more commonly-acknowledged form of narrative closure – the resolution at the end of the story of narrative enigmas.

59

Enigmas are questions set up, gaps opened up, in narratives which construct a readerly desire for plenitude and resolution. But are there any characteristic endings to narratives of sexual disguise, and if so to what extent do these endings impose closure? In the classic narrative the resolution of a story typically involves some restoration of equilibrium to the world of the fiction, a world disrupted by whatever event or situation sets the story in motion in the first place. Even classic narratives, though, vary in the degree to which closure is implied in their conclusions. If, for example, a story opens with a character assuming sexual disguise, the ultimate restoration of 'correct' dress to that character would suggest a considerable degree of closure in its resolution.

Thus, the film *Victor/Victoria* (in the final scene of which the Julie Andrews character appears wearing a dress and escorted by her boyfriend) might be regarded as more closed in its resolution than *Some Like It Hot*, in which the questions both of dress and of gender identity, certainly in relation to the Jack Lemmon character, 'Daphne', are in some respects left rather unresolved in the speedboat scene which ends the film. Nevertheless, in neither film is there ever any question of doubt on the spectator's part about the 'true' gender of sexually disguised characters. In this respect, the films' narratives are marked by a greater degree of closure than would be the case with the novel *Orlando*, say, in which the central character is never finally fixed for the reader as 'really' either male or female.

In all narratives, beginnings and endings are separated by a process, a trajectory through which each story traces its own particular path. Fictions of sexual disguise generate certain kinds of questions, specific desires that keep the story moving along its track. Dominant among these is the desire, however expressed, to fathom the appearance/essence conundrum, to lay bare the reality beneath the clothing and so settle the crucial question of who is male and who is female. Although this may be only one of several respects in which crossdressing narratives are centrally *about* gender and sexual difference, it is perhaps the most important if only because through this particular desire sexual difference is constructed in the same moment both as a question of import in a particular narrative and also as a cultural and ideological problem.

In crossdressing narratives, desire to resolve the problem of sexual difference may be embodied in certain characters in the fiction, characters set up as deceived or uncertain about the gender of another character. For example, a pivotal sequence in the film *Victor/Victoria* is constructed around the premiss that King Marchand (James Garner) is desperately keen to know whether or not Victor (Julie Andrews) is actually a boy. It is interesting, in view of the ideological conflation of subjectivity, gender and body discussed above, that Marchand's desire can apparently be gratified only by his contriving to see Victor naked. A desire to resolve the matter of sexual difference is not necessarily confined to characters within the fiction, however. The reader may be positioned in exactly this way, too, especially if the narrative solicits identification with a character who is on a quest for some sort of truth about gender identity. While in *Victor/Victoria* the spectator, unlike Marchand, knows all along that Victor is really Victoria,[6] it is nevertheless possible still to identify with Marchand's desire: to want to know whether, how, and with what consequences this character discovers the truth. Although what Marchand finally sees is not actually revealed (the reverse shot that would show his point-of-view on the crucial part of Victor/Victoria's naked body is withheld), and 'how' is detailed at some length, and in this respect the narrative finally yields to all the various components of the spectator's, as well as of Marchand's, desire.

This example highlights a property of narrativity which is of particular importance to fictions of sexual disguise: narrative point-of-view, through which readers are positioned as knowing or otherwise in relation to events in the fiction. Stories differ in the degree to which their telling, their narration, lets readers in on what is going on. In the classic narrative, the reader tends to be placed in a position of superior knowledge *vis-à-vis* characters in the story:

61

Marchand, for example, does not know whether Victor is male or female, while the spectator does. Such an all-embracing narrative point-of-view has been termed the 'view behind', its operation contrasting with a narration through which the reader is placed in a position of knowledge more-or-less equivalent to that enjoyed by characters in the fiction the 'view with'.[7] Although the narration of any one story may be marked throughout by either a 'view with' or a 'view behind', viewpoint may equally well shift within the diegesis. Narrative point-of-view constitutes another co-ordinate of openness or closure, the 'view behind' being associated with narrative closure.

In crossdressing films which, like *Victor/Victoria*, have a performance theme, the assumption of sexual disguise is usually what activates the narrative, and the narration straightaway puts spectators in a privileged position: they already know the 'truth' about the gender of disguised characters while other characters in the fiction do not. Such an advantage (never enjoyed in quite the same way by spectators of film thrillers with a crossdressing theme) must be regarded as a condition of comedy. Thus in *Some Like It Hot*, the bedtime scene on the train, for example, could work as comedy only with a narrative 'view behind'. The spectator has to know that 'Daphne' is not really a girl, and that Sugar (Marilyn Monroe) is deceived in her belief to the contrary, in order to be able to draw on the range of cultural references around courtship and sexuality that makes this particular case of mistaken identity so funny. It is funny not only because of the disparity in knowledge between Sugar and the spectator, but also because throughout the sequence the spectator is constantly being reminded of that disparity. To this extent, a measure of sadism on the spectator's part is necessary to the comic effect. Crossdressing films that are regarded as comedies are characterised by a narration which ensures that the spectator is never for an instant in doubt as to which of the characters is 'really' male and which 'really' female. The unchallenged spectator is free, from a secure vantage point, to laugh at the travesty, the comedy of errors attending the ignorance and confusion of the fiction's characters. Comedy, in this sense, does not denaturalise sexual difference.

If a 'view behind' characterises the narration of the comedy of sexual disguise, in other types of crossdressing film – notably the thriller – the spectator, far from being sure from the outset about the gender of particular characters, may at times be just as uncertain as characters within the fiction itself. A 'view with', apart from enhancing the mystery which the narrative sets out to solve, may temporarily shake the spectator's conviction that gender distinctions are absolute, and so generate anxiety and a compensating desire for a return to certainty about these matters. Despite the fact that this desire is usually in the final instance gratified, the moment of uncertainty is of some consequence.

In *Psycho*, for example, the spectator is at first not simply uncertain, but in fact deceived, as to the gender of Marion's murderer. The shadow – of what appears to be a female figure – on the shower curtain turns out to be a false clue. In this case, the narration 'knows' more than the spectator, and much of the subsequent story plays on the spectator's apparent knowledge and effective deception. Similarly in *Dressed to Kill*, during the sequence leading up to the murder of Kate in the lift, the spectator is rendered uncertain about the gender of her assailant – who is in fact later discovered to be a transsexual. In narratives which seem to offer little knowledge about what is 'really going on', the reader tends to be 'integrated into the world of the characters'.[8] When characters in the fiction are unsure about what is happening in their world, the reader is in an equally ambiguous position and must remain suspended in uncertainty or try to solve the riddle with what little information is offered. A narrative viewpoint as potentially unsettling as this typically characterises moments at least of film thrillers.

If their stories problematise gender identity and sexual difference, classic narrative films involving crossdressing aspire nevertheless to resolve the questions they raise, at least in their endings. Such films do vary, however, in the nature of their closure, in the degree to which they are closed, and consequently in their treatment of the problem of sexual difference.

Crossdressing, cinema and sexual difference

An examination of narrative organisation and narrative viewpoint usefully highlights the ways in which cinema draws on narrativity as a set of codes which cut across different forms and modes of representation. It cannot, however, address the question of the operation of cinema precisely as *cinema*, as a specific mode of representation. Throughout its history, cinematic representation has worked predominantly in the service of storytelling, and – as the foregoing discussion of characteristic narrative strategies of films of sexual disguise would suggest – films have mobilised codes of narrativity that also characterise vehicles of storytelling (the novel, for instance) other than cinema. But as a mode of representation in its own right, narrative cinema also has at its disposal a distinct set of codes which produce cinematic narrative meanings. The specificity of cinema as representation lies in its construction of spectacle – of a larger-than-life image which nonetheless also often claims if not actually to reproduce reality, at least to suspend the spectator's awareness of the artifice of the medium.

In recent years, film theorists have attempted to explore cinema's construction of its peculiar forms of visibility as pleasurable and simultaneously in some sense 'truthful'.[9] This project has involved analysing cinema's narrative discourse – cinematic enunciation – in its specificity as it incorporates visibility and solicits the involvement of the spectator. In a variety of ways, cinematic enunciation is constructed around visibility: at the same time, cinema's exercise of visibility tends to generate a narrative 'view behind', if only because the narration addresses itself precisely to the spectator's look. Point-of-view is almost literal, for knowledge is guaranteed through what can be seen.

Crossdressing films, it seems, often rely heavily on

variants of the overarching narrative viewpoint. For example, the comedy of sexual disguise depends, in order to be funny, exactly on the spectator's privileged knowledge – in this case about the gender of sexually disguised characters. Here the specifically cinematic articulation of the narrative 'view behind' is crucial. A characteristic example of how this works is provided by a sequence towards the end of *Some Like It Hot* in which 'Josephine' (Tony Curtis) kisses Sugar during the singer's act in the hotel ballroom. Unlike other characters on the scene, including Sugar herself, the spectator already knows that the 'Josephine' character is a man, and that he is very attracted to Sugar. Within the sequence itself, however, this pre-existing knowledge is sustained and reinforced by shots of 'Josephine' which offer the spectator views of the character to which it is clear that none of the film's characters is privy. Josephine/Joe is seen waiting by an entrance to the ballroom, still in drag but with wig awry, wearing no make-up and with female persona obviously dropped, looking longingly at Sugar. The defeminised appearance and the signs of masculine desire, to which the film's spectator alone is witness, serve not only as a reminder of the character's maleness, but also as a foil to the bandleader's and her sidekicks' aghast reaction when they see Sugar being kissed very passionately by another woman. This example is by no means isolated. In such a manner, 'true' gender is repeatedly made visible to the spectator, while the ignorance of certain of the film's characters – because unlike the spectator they are not in a position to see the truth – is constantly emphasised.

As spectacle, cinema does not only claim a peculiar credibility on behalf of the visible, however: in doing this, it appeals also to certain forms of pleasure. In privileging in its own ways the instance of looking, classic narrative cinema offers visual pleasure of specific kinds: through engagement of desire for pleasurable looking, the spectator is caught up with the image on the screen. The act of watching a film, it has been suggested, involves relations of looking which evoke the very processes in which the human subject is psychically constructed as fixed and gendered. If looking

65

and visual pleasure in general construct sexual difference, then so do spectator–text relations in cinema. Laura Mulvey has offered an explanation of how this process operates concretely in cinema – for example in the constitution of woman characters in films as spectacle, constructed in the image as 'to-be-looked-at' and confirmed as such not only by the spectator's gaze, but also by that of male protagonists of the fiction.[10]

Consideration of sexual difference and the look as central moments in spectator–text relations in cinema acquires a special significance with regard to crossdressing films. Such a consideration recalls, on one level, the argument already advanced that crossdressing draws upon, and reconstructs through representation, discourses around gender identity and sexual difference. More importantly, perhaps, it also brings into focus an issue of some import for representations of crossdressing which has not yet been examined in the present context: the direction of crossdressing. Given the arguments about the specificity of the construction of woman as spectacle in classic narrative cinema, the question of whether a narrative film involving sexual disguise is about male–female or female–male crossdressing acquires some significance.

Where crossdressing in films is, as seems most frequently the case, male–female, sexually disguised characters are subject to being constructed as spectacle: so that, for instance, cinematic codes through which 'real' female characters in films are routinely set up in this way – lingering close-ups, soft-focus, point-of-view shots – may be activated. But when the spectator knows that these characters in women's dress are 'really' men, this courting of the spectator's look draws attention to certain conventions of cinematic representation, and so involves the text in a degree of self-referentiality as well. Through the construction of sexually disguised male characters as objects of pleasurable looking, attention may be drawn to conventions of cinematic representation which are in ordinary circumstances so much taken-for-granted as to be invisible. Where the spectator is aware that the characters are, clothes notwithstanding, not really women, such self-referentiality heightens the comedy.

This reflexivity is nowhere more evident than in the sequence in *Some Like It Hot* in which the musicians Joe and Gerry appear for the first time in their disguise as women. Hurrying along a station platform to catch the train that will take them with Sweet Sue's band to Florida, they get a first look at their glamorous colleague-to-be, Sugar.

1

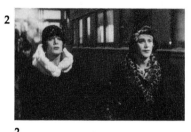

1
MLS rear view two pairs   *Music starts*
of legs below waist.
Track forward.

2

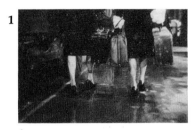

2
Medium 2-shot 'Josephine'   LOUDSPEAKER: Florida
and 'Daphne' walk along   One leaving on track one for
platform. Track back.   Washington,

3

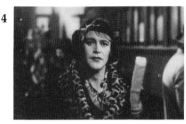

3

MCU 'Josephine'. Track back.	. . . Charleston, Jackson and Miami. All aboard!

4

MCU 'Daphne'. Track back. . . . All aboard!

5 MLS rear view as 1 to LS.
  D stumbles and looks back. D: Ow! *Music stops*

6 Medium 2-shot J and D as 2.
  They stop. J: What's the matter now?
  D: How do they walk in
  these things? How do they
  keep their balance?
  J: Must be the way the
  weight's distributed.

  They start walking. Now come on!
  Track back. D: It's so draughty. They
  must be catching cold all the
  time, huh?
  J: Will you quit stalling?

  They stop. We're gonna miss the train.
  D: I feel naked. I feel like
  everybody's staring at me.

They stop and look.

7 LS girls in the band line
up to board train.

8 Medium 2-shot J and D as 6.

J: With those legs? Are you
crazy? Now come on!
D: Uh-oh!

Female chatter

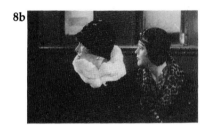

8b

D: It's no use, we're not
gonna get away with it, Joe.
J: The name is Josephine,
and this was your idea in the
first place.

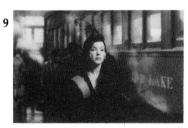

9

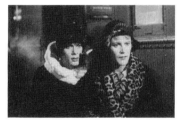

9a
MCU Sugar. Track back.
S walks past J and D who
turn and stare after her,
offscreen right.

9b
Music starts

10

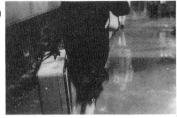

10
MCU rear view S's legs from below waist to LS. Steam shoots from train, S stumbles and looks back. Runs to join band.

Music ends

11

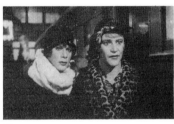

11
Medium 2-shot J and D as 9b, staring offscreen right.

D: Look at that! Look how she moves! It's just like Jello on springs. Must have some sort of built-in motor or something. I tell ya, it's a whole different sex!
J: What are you afraid of? Nobody's asking you to have a baby. This is just to get us out of town. Once we get to Florida, we'll blow this whole setup.
D: Joe, this time I am not going to let you talk me into something that . . .

Looking, in fact, is precisely what is at stake here. This short sequence of less than two minutes, in introducing Sugar, 'Josephine' and 'Daphne' as, in a sense, 'new' characters, marks a major move forward in the film's narrative and sets up a series of significant analogies and distinctions. On one level, the visual treatment of both Sugar and the Josephine/Daphne duo evokes some of the conventions by which classic narrative cinema constructs female characters as objects of the spectator's look. The first shot, for example, offers a voyeuristic view of legs and behinds which in cultural terms would suggest that the objects of the camera's gaze are female. At the same time, a rear view of this kind obviously withholds the identity of the owners of the legs (though the stumble would perhaps offer a retrospective clue). But any suspense is in any case shortlived, because the problem of identity is solved in the next three shots: the legs belong to Joe and Gerry, now in drag. In these shots, too, the signification of the conventionally female clothes and make-up worn by the characters is underscored by the fact that, in cinematic terms, they are effectively 'feminised', notably in the lingering individual close-ups of shots 3 and 4.

These first shots of Josephine and Daphne are formally similar to shot 10 and the opening of shot 9, in which Sugar makes her first appearance. But there is nevertheless one highly significant difference between these rhyming sets of shots. In the Josephine/Daphne series, the point-of-view is that of the camera. The camera, in other words, is the enunciator: it tells the story. Both shots of Sugar, by contrast, are point-of-view shots, motivated by the looks of Josephine and Daphne. Shot 8, for example, which precedes the first view of Sugar, ends on the two disguised musicians gazing offscreen left, so that shot 9 – our first sight of Sugar – clearly at least begins as a point-of-view shot (although this shot is interesting in that point-of-view shifts within it away from the characters and back to the camera). When, as here, the spectator's look coincides with that of characters in the fiction, the source of enunciation is both camera and characters.

Search
eor

This coincidence of point-of-view also occurs in shot 10, a rear view of Sugar whose composition is similar to that of the first shot of the sequence: this time, however, the view is motivated by the goggle-eyed stares of Josephine and Daphne which end shot 9. This pair of shots is confirmed as a point-of-view sequence when bracketed by shot 11, which repeats the end of shot 9 and underscores the centrality of the look in the dialogue:

> *Daphne:* Look at that! Look how she moves! . . . I
> tell ya, its a whole different sex!

Daphne's exclamation serves also as a reminder of how looking functions in the construction of sexual difference. For in this sequence is neatly condensed a complex interplay of cinematic codes which construct difference through cinematic enunciation and spectacle. On the one hand, Josephine and Daphne, pretending to be women, seem to receive the same sort of visual treatment as the 'real' woman, Sugar. At the same time, however, the shifts of point-of-view between the camera on one side and Josephine/Daphne on the other mark these characters as masculine. For if it is true that in classic cinema looks within the diegesis tend to originate with male characters, an identity of character and camera in a point-of-view shot is readable as a masculine identification.

Here the rhyming of shots, and the simultaneous undercutting of the rhyme by shifts of point-of-view, call attention to the cinematic conventions through which women are constructed as 'to-be-looked-at', while at the same time affirming the difference between the 'real' woman and the counterfeits. Moreover, in appealing to their prior knowledge of both narrative viewpoint and conventions of cinematic representation, this sequence constructs spectators precisely as *knowing*: knowing about the artifice not only of cinema but also of conventional signs of gender identity. For the knowing spectator – and in this case all spectators are addressed as knowing – irony and comedy are interpolated in layers of self-referentiality.

But what of another argument advanced by Mulvey: that

in spectator–text relations in cinema the look operates in one of its aspects to disavow the castration threat posed, culturally, by woman's body?[11] This fetishistic look, by idealising and empowering woman, asserts that she is, after all, phallic, that there is no threat of castration. In films like *Some Like it Hot* and *Tootsie*, male characters disguised as women – performers in 'real life' as much as in the story – may be constructed as objects of fetishistic looking. But since in these cases the spectator knows that these 'women' really are phallic, the reassurance offered by a fetishised image is redundant. Although it may operate on one level to enhance the self-referentiality of the crossdressing comedy, there is perhaps more to the idealised image than simply this. It is possible that such a spectacle also fulfils the primal fantasy of the fetishistic look, a fantasy which 'real' women must always frustrate: it banishes the castration threat by gratifying a masculine desire for a woman to be, in one fundamental respect, more like a man. Film critics have suggested that Dustin Hoffman's Dorothy Michaels in *Tootsie* comes across not only as a better person than her 'real' alter ego Michael Dorsey, but also as a better woman than any of the 'real' women in the film. In looking at Dorothy on the screen, the spectator's privileged knowledge of the truth *of* the artifice as well as the truth *behind* the artifice confirms this. In such narratives of sexual disguise, cinema asserts quite firmly that the body beneath the clothes is indeed the ultimate site of sexual difference, and that the difference is after all absolute. At the same time, though, does it not also offer a softly whispered comment upon its own capacity to deliver such bold assurances?

4

The Big Sleep: censorship, film text and sexuality

An approach to reading representations which confines itself to the formal characteristics of images and texts may be extremely productive, but can hardly be regarded as exhaustive. A text is obviously instrumental in producing its own meanings, but meaning nonetheless always exceeds the limits of any one text: readings are always informed by various contexts and intertexts. So, for instance, films of sexual disguise would in effect be unreadable without some familiarity on the audience's part with cultural meanings attaching to social practices of crossdressing.

The following essay, which focusses on Howard Hawks's film *The Big Sleep*, may be read as a recipe for combining textual analysis with a certain sort of contextual investigation. However, it moves beyond the ideological/cultural contexts appealed to in the previous chapter's consideration of films of sexual disguise to enter the terrain of social, historical and industrial contexts. In this sense, the essay attempts a broadening of methodological perspective. Though in another sense, too, in concentrating on certain features of the industrial context of production of one particular film, its focus is relatively specific. In attempting to come to terms with questions of context whilst holding at the same time to a model of the film text as productive of meaning in its own right, the arguments advanced here are directed towards constructing a method for dealing in tandem with film texts

74

and their social, historical and industrial contexts.

This work was conceived in a seminar on Film Criticism which I taught for one semester in an American university. Alongside the study of various strands of film theory, the class was engaged in an ongoing analytical project on *The Big Sleep*, chosen largely because of my own fascination with the film's famed impenetrability. In line with the topic of the seminar, the emphasis here was on a formalist approach to the film's internal textual operations. This proved a very effective method of teaching film theory: it enlivened the (sometimes difficult) theory that had to be understood, developed basic skills of film analysis, was highly pleasurable in itself, and produced tangible and gratifying results for all concerned, teacher as well as students.

It is to the Film Criticism seminar that I owe the impetus behind this chapter: for a concentrated exposure to textual analysis rapidly promotes as much awareness of the limitations as of the usefulness of the method. Even – or especially – a surface reading of *The Big Sleep* yields a morass of contradiction, inconsistency and 'disturbance in the sphere of sexuality': and the Freudian notion of censorship seems to fit very well as a description of what, textually speaking, is going on. In this project, the shift between text and context is provoked by a play of words, a double meaning around 'censorship', more than by any profound methodological or theoretical break. Censorship, of course, is also a set of institutional practices: the concept consequently suggests a possible point of *rapprochement* between a film text and certain aspects of its production context. The analysis advanced in this chapter follows on from such a link.

The initial motivation for this project, then, was a combination of a pedagogical imperative and a desire to penetrate the mystery that is *The Big Sleep*. At a more general level, a textual/contextual analysis such as this one aspires to be may be justified in two ways. Firstly, since textual analysis involves taking apart the codes which construct a film, it may be regarded as a necessary first step in acquiring understanding of how one particular culturally dominant form of representation – Hollywood narrative cinema – works. The political implications of such an enterprise are noted elsewhere (see the introduction to Chapter 1). Secondly, the analysis put forward here may be read in the context of the discipline of film studies. In broaching the relationship between text and context without assuming either that the one is always an effect of the other, or that they operate entirely independently of each other, this chapter offers itself as a contribution towards the development of a particular kind of theoretically-informed film history.

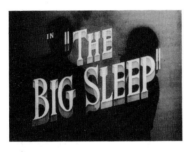

Private detective Philip Marlowe is called in by dying millionaire General Sternwood to investigate a case of blackmail involving his degenerate daughter, Carmen, and Arthur Gwynn Geiger, who calls himself a dealer in rare books. Sternwood is also concerned about the disappearance of his erstwhile employee and companion, Shawn Regan. Vivian Rutledge, Sternwood's divorced elder daughter, wishes to protect Carmen from the consequences of her vices, but is herself in some way involved with Eddie Mars, a big-time gambler. Geiger is murdered, and this sets in train a series of crimes, including several more killings, among them that of Eddie Mars. In the course of all this, Marlowe and Vivian fall in love.

I

The Big Sleep, a film based on the 1939 novel by Raymond

Chandler and directed by Howard Hawks, has a reputation for being immensely enjoyable but – as far as its story goes – quite obscure.[1] On its release in 1946, *New York Times* film critic Bosley Crowther called *The Big Sleep* 'one of those pictures in which so many cryptic things occur amid so much involved and devious plotting that the mind becomes utterly confused. . . . [T]he complex of blackmail and murder soon becomes a web of utter bafflement'.[2] Crowther might have been the first to find the film confusing, but he was certainly not the last. Tales abound of how, for instance, Hawks – and even Chandler himself – were unable to figure out who does what to whom and why in *The Big Sleep*. Hawks is alleged to have wired Chandler during the shooting of the film to ask who was responsible for one of the six murders, that of the Sternwoods' chauffeur Owen Taylor. Chandler could reputedly offer no answer. And yet Hawks himself has said of the film: 'It's told from the point of view of the detective and there are no red herrings'. Examination of the film reveals that Hawks is correct on both counts. So why the confusion?

Indeed, *The Big Sleep* is quite a mystery. In the sense that it is about the investigation by a detective–hero of a series of crimes, its narrative is exemplary of the 1940s mystery/*film noir* genre. But the film itself constitutes something of a puzzle, too, and the oft-remarked 'confusing' quality of its narrative offers its own challenge – to unravel what 'really' happens in the story: the narrative of the film consequently becomes a topic of investigation in its own right. But how confusing is it, really? Close study suggests that at the level of narrative, the film's renowned confusion is more apparent than real. In a model for the structural analysis of narratives developed in *Morphology of the Folktale* by the Russian Formalist Vladimir Propp, the basic unit of narrativity, or narrative 'function', is taken to be 'the act of *dramatis personae* . . . defined from the point of view of its signifi-cance for the course of the action of the tale as a whole'.[3] Folktale narratives are composed of a limited set of functions, each of them named and categorised by Propp; they proceed according to a circumscribed number of narrative 'moves', from an initial 'villainy' or 'lack' which sets the story in motion to the wedding of hero and princess, or its functional equivalent, which typically closes the story. Surprisingly perhaps, Hollywood film narratives have proved quite susceptible to this type of structural analysis.[4]

A Proppian analysis of *The Big Sleep*, for instance, reveals that there is a high degree of closure in the film's narrative, in that only one of its moves remains finally unresolved. Such an analysis also reveals, however, that this narrative is marked by a large number of delays and retardations. These generally take the form of an imbrication of functions from different narrative moves, so that the resolution of each move is delayed by irruption of elements of the narrative which do not 'belong' within that particular move (see Table 4.1).[5] This may be one of the sources of 'confusion' in the film. Since, however, it seems that such a structure of imbrication and retardation could well be regarded as typical of the detective/investigative narrative as a genre, I would not regard this as a sufficient explanation of the 'obscurity' of one particular detective story.

If the 'confusing' character of *The Big Sleep*'s narrative is indeed more apparent than real, we have another mystery on our hands: why are allegations of unfathomability so frequent and so repetitive? Why, for instance, is the story of the Hawks-Chandler telegram retold in almost everything written about the film, particularly when there is no real evidence of its veracity? All this begins to suggest itself as symptomatic. Symptomatic of what, though? To address oneself to symptoms in this way is to argue for a certain kind of analysis of the discourse producing the symptoms, in this instance a film text. However, analysis which starts, stays the course, and finishes with a film text can unravel only part of the mystery. It is important also to take into account elements of the film's social/historical context, and certainly the immediate institutional conditions of its production. The relationship between text and context has particular relevance with regard to questions raised by *The Big Sleep*. The film's allegedly confusing character may be regarded as an outcome of various operations of censorship. Censorship is understood here in at least two senses, and in such a way that analysis of the film may open up the possibility of bringing together work on the text with work on the context of its production.

As textual body, *The Big Sleep*, I would argue, is crucially constituted by a work of censorship. Censorship may be seen both as an unconscious operation which structures the film text, and also as the textual effect or residue of a set of institutions and practices operating at the level of the film's material production. Although there may be a problem in establishing the nature of the relationship between these two moments of censorship within the operation of the film text, it is evident that at both levels censorship is a *productive* operation rather than, as it is commonly conceived, a process of excision, of cutting things out. A look at *The Big Sleep* from the point of view of censorship reveals that the text is not merely marked, but is positively structured, by the operations of censorship, or censorships. Censorships, in an important sense, produce this text.

II

Film censorship is often understood as a conscious process of determining, at the level of content, what does, or more usually does not, go into films. So defined, censorship usually takes place within, and is legitimated by, institutions which possess a certain conventional or legal authority. From this point of view, the film *The Big Sleep* may usefully be compared with the novel from which it was adapted, and the sources of any differences between the two looked into. In fact, a rather complicated production history marks *The Big Sleep*'s passage from Chandler novel to Howard Hawks film.[6] It began in late August 1944 when Hawks, working with Warner Brothers, assigned the writing of a scenario based on Raymond Chandler's novel to William Faulkner. Faulkner shared the work with novice scriptwriter Leigh Brackett and they worked on alternate chapters of the book,

Table 4.1 Analysis of narrative of *The Big Sleep*

1st move	2nd move	3rd move	4th move
villainy: Geiger's blackmail note to Sternwood			
killing of enemy without a fight: Marlowe finds Geiger murdered	*villainy*: Geiger's murder		
Liquidation of villainy: Geiger can no longer blackmail Sternwoods			
		lack: Geiger's body missing	
	killing of enemy without a fight: Owen Taylor found dead in car		*villainy*: Taylor's murder
			THIS MOVE REMAINS UNRESOLVED
		liquidation of lack: Marlowe finds Geiger's body	
	liquidation of villainy: Marlowe verbalises his conclusion that Taylor murdered Geiger		

5th move	6th move	7th move
		lack: Shawn Regan is missing
		reconnaissance: Vivian asks to see Marlowe
		reconnaissance: Marlowe takes Carmen home and sees Vivian
villainy: Vivian blackmailed with photos of Carmen		
struggle with villain: Marlowe's verbal battle with Brody		
object of search handed over: Brody gives Marlowe the photos		
	villainy: Brody's murder	
	fight in an open field: Marlowe and Lundgren fight	
	object of search handed over: Lundgren turned in to police	
		reconnaissance: Marlowe meets Vivian at restaurant
		lack: Marlowe verbalises his lack of knowledge to Bernie Ohls, the policeman
		skirmishes with villainous donors: Marlowe beaten up by hoods, later by Canino
		fight in an open field: Marlowe confronts and kills Canino
		struggle with villain, victory in contest: Marlowe confronts Eddie Mars
		liquidation of lack: Marlowe tells Vivian what befell Shawn Regan.
		Wedding: Marlowe and Vivian together

81

producing a 'temporary screenplay' within a matter of eight days. This they expanded into a final screenplay or shooting script, which was finished by the end of September.

Even at this early stage, certain things in the novel are already absent from the film scenario. During the 1940s, the US film industry's self-regulation through a system of prior censorship administered by a department of the film producers' body, the Motion Picture Association of America (MPAA), accounted for upwards of 95 per cent of all films exhibited in the USA. The Production Code Administration of the MPAA was, as its name indicates, responsible for the administration of the Hollywood Production Code, a document setting out various prohibitions and warnings concerning the content of motion pictures, and supporting these strictures with moral arguments. The PCA vetted film projects at all stages of production, from initial ideas through to finished films, in accordance with Production Code guidelines. All the major studios had departments responsible for liaising with the PCA, and Faulkner and Brackett may have been instructed by the appropriate department at Warner Brothers to omit any reference to the 'illegal drug traffic', to 'sex perversion', and to 'complete nudity',[7] all of which feature in Chandler's *The Big Sleep*. Accordingly not only, for example, are Geiger's pornographic book racket, Carmen's drug taking and Geiger's homosexuality never explicitly mentioned in the film, they were actually written out at the very earliest stage of its production.

Shooting of *The Big Sleep* began on 10 October 1944, with a forty-two-day schedule. However, just as shooting was about to begin, the Faulkner-Brackett final scene in the script was rejected by the PCA. In this scene, Marlowe is shown to be indirectly responsible for Carmen's death, something not to be brooked in a hero figure. The PCA made some suggestions for alterations, and the script was further modified by Hawks, Jules Furthman (the third credited writer) and, briefly, Faulkner again. In the film, Carmen does not actually die but is instead sent away (*Marlowe*: 'They have places for that. Maybe they can cure her. It's been done before'). Hawks and Furthman (together, it seems, with a six-foot-two chorus girl called 'Stuttering Sam') rewrote various parts of the script during actual shooting. These rewrites mainly affected the second half of the script and were devoted largely to developing the Marlowe–Vivian relationship. Shooting was completed thirty-four days behind schedule on 12 January 1945.

During Summer 1945, the resulting version of *The Big Sleep* was previewed to US servicemen abroad, apparently a common practice at the time. In late January 1946, some of the cast were called back for the shooting of some retakes and new scenes, all devoted to the further enhancement of the Marlowe–Vivian romance: scenes between the couple in a restaurant and in Vivian's bedroom were among those shot at this stage. The film's stars, Humphrey Bogart and Lauren Bacall, had in the interim married each other, and the film became something of a celebration of their real-life romance.

In its revised version, *The Big Sleep* was finally released in August 1946 in the US and in October 1946 in Britain, some two years after it was first begun. This two-year period saw a series of transformations between novel and film, not all of them the result of institutional censorship. The process of adaptation from a written to a visual medium in itself demands differences of approach, though Chandler's novel is so spare and its dialogue so sharp that Faulkner's and Brackett's original script remains very close not only in spirit, but often also word-for-word, to Chandler's novel – except, that is, for the changes demanded *a priori* by the Production Code. The PCA's subsequent request for a different ending is a nod in the direction of the 'compensating moral values' called for in the Code. While the mere mention of, say, drugs or pornography was absolutely prohibited, characters could quite freely be shot and beaten up on screen provided the perpetrators of such acts were clearly shown to be villains.

Other transformations between novel and film have more to do with the Hollywood system and the authorial marks of Hawks than with institutional film censorship. But in the film's final scene, the imperatives of institutional censorship, star system and 'Hawksian' codes intersect with, and overdetermine, each other: Marlowe, as hero, remains (within the terms of the Production Code) morally unimpeachable; Bogart and Bacall are about to fall into one another's arms; and Vivian and Marlowe prove themselves to be an exemplary Hawksian team – witty, resourceful, mutually supportive and, above all, 'good' (*Marlowe* to *Vivian*: 'I didn't have a chance to thank you for what you did back there. You looked good, awful good').

III

As film text, *The Big Sleep* bears the marks of its contexts, of its various institutional conditions of production. These contexts *effect* the text, in that they are productive of meanings within it. Overlaid on an investigatory narrative in which a detective–hero seeks for 'truth' in the shadowy world of *film noir* is the trajectory of a heterosexual romance informed by the Hollywood star system's intertext. An unspeakable, because institutionally censored, subtext underlies both, though in the *noir* world this begins to hover on the brink of articulation.

The film falls fairly cleanly into two sections corresponding respectively, and more-or-less neatly, with *film noir* and heterosexual romance elements. Studio publicity in the form of the Warner Brothers trailer for *The Big Sleep*, presenting 'in 90 seconds the material that films will take 90 minutes to work over',[8] foregrounds the dual structure of the film:

> *Marlowe* (voice-over): . . . that house that stood alone in the shadows' . . . There's something more dangerous, more deadly than I'd ever known before in that room. . . .
> CUT to Vivian and Marlowe, kissing.
> *Vivian*: I'd like more.
> CAPTION: They're together again!

The 'deadliness' of female sexuality implied in this juxta-position of shots condenses *film noir* conventions, the heterosexual romance and its star system intertext, and the operations of the film's subtext.

The two parts of *The Big Sleep* are approximately equal in terms of running time. The transition between parts one and two occurs after a scene in which Marlowe overpowers the killer of blackmailer Joe Brody, Geiger's 'shadow' Carol Lundgren, and hands Lundgren over to the police. It is marked by a lengthy fade to a scene in a restaurant where Marlowe meets Vivian Rutledge and challenges her for the first time with a question which he will subsequently repeat more than once: 'What's Eddie Mars got on you?' As far as the narrative is concerned, most of the villainies which set the story in train take place, or are established as having already taken place, in part one: two blackmail attempts, Shawn Regan's disappearance, three of the six murders. Each of these villainies constitutes a puzzle whose solution is put forward as necessary to narrative closure both for Marlowe and for the film's spectator. This is established in a *mise-en-scène* which positions the detective as enunciator, in sole command of the narrative (or, as Hawks would have it, the story is told from the point of view of the detective). Marlowe's position in relation to the puzzles set up by the narrative is thus identical with the spectator's.

In the second part of the film, the preoccupation with a series of enigmas to be investigated, decoded and recon-structed in the form of a verbally-articulated 'truth' gets displaced onto the progress of a heterosexual romance – the relationship between Marlowe and Vivian. This relationship develops through a series of 'reconnaissances' (to use Propp's term) which function to delay on the one hand the solution of the enigmas and on the other the consummation of the relationship between the couple. The one thus becomes a condition of the other: Marlowe cannot recon-struct the 'truth' of the matter in hand until he has solved the additional enigma posed by Vivian (repeatedly articulated as 'What's Eddie Mars got on you?'). Nor will any resolution of the relationship be on the cards until he can finally wrest back from Vivian command of the enunciation of 'truth'. Thus, while the first part of the film sets up the disruptions which motivate the narrative, the second in effect constitutes a substantial retardation device by means of which narrative closure is held off through a displacement of the enigmas set up in part one onto, and their condensation in, the question: 'What's Eddie Mars got on you?'

Further internal evidence may be advanced in support of the argument that the film narrative divides itself precisely into these two parts. A Proppian analysis, for example, shows that the narrative is made up of seven 'moves' (see Table 4.1), the first six constituting the first part of the film. The seventh, and 'major' move is coterminous more-or-less with the second part of the film.[9] It involves the enigmas set up by the figure of – and Vivian's involvement with – Eddie Mars, and the simultaneous resolution of both in the death of Mars and the implied reconciliation of Marlowe and Vivian at the end of the film.

> *Vivian*: You've forgotten one thing. Me.
> *Marlowe*: What's wrong with you?
> *Vivian*: Nothing you can't fix.

IV

The two parts of *The Big Sleep* are clearly marked off from each other, therefore, in terms of both narrative structure and narrative trajectory. However, the first part of the film distinguishes itself from the second also by virtue of its embodiment of a subtext of censored representations. As I have shown, certain strands in the novel could not, because of Hollywood's institutional censorship, be 'spoken' in the film. At the same time, here is a film which is repetitively labelled 'confusing', despite the fact that close study of its narrative suggests that such confusion is, to say the least, overstated. If the film's narrative is in fact intelligible, then institutional censorship cannot be taken as a sufficient explanation of its apparent confusion. We must dig deeper. Although *The Big Sleep*'s reputation as a baffling film may be in some way symptomatic, this is not to say that the symptoms are without foundation. Perhaps the film constructs a rhetoric of confusion or produces signifiers of confusion as it were unconsciously, but working on 'real' material? Such a rhetoric of confusion might then be regarded as an expression of unconscious textual processes, and analysed by treating the film text as analogous to the discourse of an analysand.

A concept of censorship which may be of relevance to the present investigation has in fact been developed in psychoanalytic theory. Freud used the term censorship to refer to the operation whereby unconscious thoughts which may not, for whatever reason, be directly admitted to consciousness are subject to distortion in the production of the analysand's observable discourse or symptoms. Censorship in this sense has been discussed a good deal in relation to dreams, though it is argued that similar processes are also at work in the production of neurotic symptoms. In the case of the dream-work, a wish or dream-thought which is in some way repugnant is expressed in the dream in altered form: as such, distortion imposed by the censorship constitutes a primary revision of the dream-thought. The more obscure or puzzling a dream or symptom appears, says Freud, the more powerful has been the work of the censorship. Blanks, gaps, inconsistencies and distortions – precisely 'confusions' – serve the analyst as evidence that censorship has taken place.

It is evident that a fairly straightforward analogy with conscious processes of literary and journalistic censorship is being advanced here:

> According to the strength and sensitiveness of the censorship he [sic; the writer] finds himself compelled either merely to refrain from certain forms of attack or to speak in allusions in place of direct references, or he must conceal his objectionable pronouncements beneath some apparently innocent disguise.[10]

Although this is exactly an analogy, and the processes of

unconscious censorship are different from those of institutional censorship, the outcomes of each may be similar, and even overdetermined. If unconscious censorship is at work in *The Big Sleep*, we are faced with the problem of determining its motivation or origin. To what extent are the apparent gaps and confusions of the film the effects of a work of censorship as unconscious textual operation? And what purpose would be served by such a censorship in the film?

If the 'confusion' of *The Big Sleep* melts away on close inspection of its narrative, perhaps investigation might more fruitfully be directed elsewhere, for instance at the film's *mise-en-scène* (the contents of the film frame: settings, costumes, composition of the image and movement within frame). That which cannot be overtly expressed in the narrative may express itself indirectly within the plurality of visual codes of cinema. If the *mise-en-scène* of *The Big Sleep* is marked by the distortions, excesses and obscurities advanced by Freud as traces of the work of censorship in the production of dreams and other symptomatic discourses, we may take it that something is going on that could well repay a little private investigation of our own.

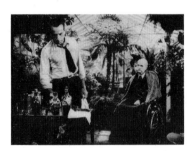

In the second scene of *The Big Sleep* Marlowe meets the ailing General Sternwood, who engages the detective to investigate Geiger's attempt to blackmail him. In this scene (significantly, Sternwood's only appearance in the film), the old man's sickness may be read as evidence of, even as punishment for, a life of unbridled and degenerate sexuality (*Sternwood*: 'You are looking, sir, at a very dull survival of a very gaudy life'). The relationship between the exotic (here Sternwood's hothouse and the orchids) and the degenerate are established early in the film, and fairly overtly, at the levels of both *mise-en-scène* and dialogue. As Marlowe sweats in an artificial jungle of tropical plants, Sternwood says of his orchids: 'Their flesh is too much like the flesh of men. Their perfume has the rotten sweetness of corruption.' Sternwood's hothouse, which in the film – unlike the novel – is actually attached to his house, can be read as a parallel of the film's other exotic and closed-in place, Geiger's house. Both may be regarded as displaced and condensed representations of the perverse or degenerate forms of sexuality and the consequent fragmentation of the family that it becomes a task of the narrative to try to set to rights.

Just as Sternwood is a widower who embarked on fatherhood late in life and whose daughters are, in Marlowe's words, 'both pretty, and both pretty wild', so Geiger and his 'shadow' Carol Lundgren are homosexual lovers. In both cases, the monogamous heterosexual family is either incomplete or distorted. The heterosexual promiscuity of the Sternwoods and the homosexual liaison of Geiger and Lundgren remain implicit, however, at the level of the film's narrative action. The only 'normal' relationship in the film is that between Marlowe and Vivian, and as already suggested, part of the narrative work of the film's second part is to bring these two characters together. Even here, though, the extent to which 'normality' is fully recuperated in the film's closure remains highly questionable.

The first part of *The Big Sleep* may be seen as producing a 'disturbance in the sphere of sexuality' (to adopt Freud's description of the origin of his patient Dora's hysteria) which is counterbalanced, though only partly so, by the trajectory of the Vivian–Marlowe courtship in the second part. Marlowe functions as discoverer and articulator of the 'truth'. In the detective's mouth lies the power to speak the truth and so solve the mystery and bring the narrative to a close. Vivian, on the other hand, is not only associated with the degenerate Sternwoods, she also functions as withholder of the truth and therefore as delayer of narrative closure.

This suggests an imbalance in the heterosexual sphere, which in turn indicates that the disturbance in the area of sexuality which troubles the first part of *The Big Sleep* involves not only homosexuality and heterosexual promiscuity, but female sexuality as well.

Close examination of the *mise-en-scène* of Geiger's house and of Marlowe's position within that *mise-en-scène* provides evidence in support of this. Several aspects of Geiger's house are significant in this context. First of all, like the classic 'scene of the crime', the house is a site of obsessive return: after his first visit there, Marlowe goes back no less than four times. It is noteworthy too that four out of these five visits take place in the first part of the film, while the single return there in the second part is in fact the film's closing scene, in the course of which the 'truth' of the narrative is verbally reconstructed (more-or-less) by Marlowe. None of the visits apart from the first is in fact functionally necessary to the narrative. The repetitive return to the scene of the crime may be viewed as excessive, and thus as symptomatic, therefore. Secondly, in each of the visits to Geiger's, the means of getting there – usually cars – are not merely indicated but are quite prominently foregrounded in the film image. The fact that it is always made so abundantly clear that ground has to be covered in order to arrive at the scene of the crime marks it as beyond the bounds of the everyday, of knowable and familiar time and space. Thirdly, Geiger's house is the site of a series of enigmas set up in relation to the initial villainy of the narrative – Geiger's attempt to blackmail General Sternwood.

All of these enigmas are posed within the *mise-en-scène* of the first visit to Geiger's. In the course of that first visit, Marlowe discovers Geiger's body, a camera concealed in a statuette of a head, Carmen Sternwood 'as high as a kite', and Geiger's coded 'sucker list' of blackmail victims – all in a sequence almost entirely lacking in dialogue and involving takes of a duration and camera movement of a fluidity extraordinary in relation to the rest of the film, and certainly to the Hawks *oeuvre* in general. The unusual features of this scene suggest once more that the *mise-en-scène* of Geiger's

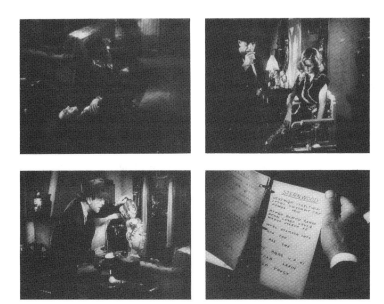

house produces meanings which exceed the function of the house either for the film's narrative or for its characterisation. Geiger's house, cut off from the daylight world of the familiar, is the classic 'other scene' – the site exactly of mystery and enigma. It is shadowy, closed-in, cluttered and messy – the *mise-en-scène* of the Unconscious, of Freud's Uncanny, at once both familiar and alien, reassuring and threatening.[11]

As well as being the end point of a series of journeys, Geiger's house is the object of a scrutinising gaze – Marlowe's, and through Marlowe the spectator's. The gaze seeks to unravel the mysteries, solve the riddles, of the house. The *mise-en-scène* of Geiger's house, in other words, offers itself as a puzzle demanding to be solved. The puzzle takes the condensed and displaced form of the 'sucker list' which Marlowe must remove from the other scene and take home in order to decode. The puzzle is none other than the riddle of the feminine.

In the first part of *The Big Sleep*, it is Vivian's sister Carmen who functions as repository of the menacing

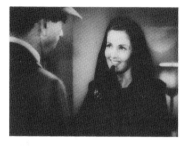 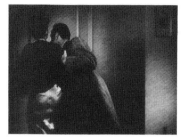

aspects of feminine sexuality, with its threat of castration and disruption of the patriarchal order. Carmen is associated with the enigmatic *mise-en-scène* of Geiger's house (Marlowe discovers her there, drugged; she has witnessed Geiger's murder; and Vivian is blackmailed as a consequence). Moreover, her infantilism has already been established in the film: instead of providing Marlowe with answers to his questions, she simply 'sucks her thumb and looks coy'. In effect, she cannot speak – like a baby. At the same time as being thus placed outside language, and so outside the Symbolic order of patriarchy, Carmen also manages, certainly as far as Marlowe is concerned, to be for the most part duplicitous. In her single appearance in the second part of the film (when she makes an unannounced visit to Marlowe's apartment), Marlowe says that her reply to his question about Eddie Mars might be 'the truth, for a change'.

Hitherto in her refusal to speak she has in effect been deceiving Marlowe by blocking his goal of obtaining and recounting the 'truth' by means of his power over language. But despite her brief moment of truthfulness, Carmen is not in the end recuperated for the Symbolic order: her punishment for functioning outside the patriarchal law is literally to be kicked out of the film's *mise-en-scène*. Vivian's fate, on the other hand, is to be recuperated into it and disarmed: initially through her own facility with language, but finally by yielding to Marlowe – the 'private dick on a case', the private eye with the penetrating gaze – her own power to withhold the truth through a duplicitous command of language.

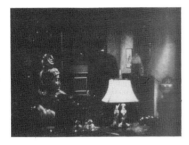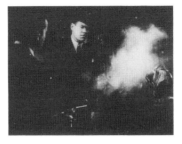

In his first visit to Geiger's, and in the course of his wordless examination of the scene he discovers there, Marlowe finds an oriental statuette of a head inside which is concealed a camera, with which – as it subsequently transpires – some photographs of Carmen, which could constitute an embarrassment to the Sternwoods if made public, have been taken. The statuette is never explicitly referred to by Marlowe nor by any other character in the film, yet its unspoken and unspeaking presence in the *mise-en-scène* is strongly marked. Given the centrality of Geiger's *mise-en-scène*, the prominent place of the statue within it would on its own serve as a clue, an indication that it is in some way significant. This is further emphasised by the central position it occupies in the composition and framing of virtually all of the shots in which it appears, and even more by the fact that during the film's final sequence it is smashed to pieces by Marlowe's gunfire.

The statue seems to be a representation of a woman. It/she obviously cannot speak, but 'sees' the murder of Geiger and so holds the key to the riddle which Marlowe must fathom. Like Carmen, the head is punished for its silence, for holding out on the hero: it is destroyed by Marlowe, just as he has kicked Carmen out of his apartment and out of the film. It is significant that the film's existing final scene replaces one originally scripted, but institutionally censored, in which Carmen is killed. In this sense as well, then, the statuette functions as a stand-in for the absent Carmen and what she represents. Both Carmen and the statue signify the menacing riddle of female sexuality with which neither Marlowe nor the film text, nor indeed the patriarchal order, can deal in any way other than with violence.

Elements of the *mise-en-scène* of *The Big Sleep*, therefore, particularly in the first part of the film, embody in distorted form elements displaced from, and unspoken and unspeakable within, the narrative. The clues – or symptoms – are to be found mainly in the representation of Geiger's house, 'the scene of the crime'. Not only is this the site of Geiger's murder and of various other activities transgressive of institutional law, its *mise-en-scène* also constitutes a symptomatic representation of sexualities which, transgressing the law of patriarchy, are not consciously speakable in the text. To the extent that the *mise-en-scène* of *The Big Sleep* bears the traces of the unrepresentable, then, it produces evidence of an unconscious work of censorship in the film text.

V

The 'disturbance in the sphere of sexuality' troubling *The Big Sleep* is symptomatically expressed within the film's generally rather sparse and functional *mise-en-scène*. The degeneracy pervading the film takes the form of various kinds of 'abnormal' – perverted, excessive or threatening – sexuality. These are not for the most part explicitly articulated in the text. On one level, of course, the absence of such representations has its source within institutional practices of film censorship – the Hollywood film industry's conscious regulation of the contents of its own products. The subtext of *The Big Sleep* must be understood, in some measure at least, as a displacement of the effects of institutional censorship.

The Production Code and the efforts of the Production Code Administration were directed predominantly at narrative themes and dialogue, though, leaving visual cinematic codes as a site onto which prohibited representations could at times, consciously or otherwise, be displaced. But institutional censorship is only one of a series of contexts which structure and mark the operation of – which *produce* –

the film text. While the *mise-en-scène* of Geiger's house may, in one sense, be regarded as a product of Hollywood's self-censorship, it is also produced, for example, by generic conventions associated with *film noir mise-en-scène* which were well established by the mid-1940s. At the contextual level, that is, the *mise-en-scène* of *The Big Sleep* must be regarded as overdetermined.

It is overdetermined at other levels, too, however. The various contexts of the film's production do not completely account for *The Big Sleep*'s subtext. There is an excess, something extra, whose explanation has to be sought elsewhere. Why, for instance, is Geiger's house the site of such compulsive return? Why are its enigmas so prominently foregrounded? How does the highly marked but entirely unspoken presence of the statuette function? The *mise-en-scène* of Geiger's house figures in the film as a discourse across which may be read a series of displaced and condensed representations of an underlying and unexpressed perversity or menace in the area of sexuality. Homosexuality and heterosexual promiscuity feature overtly in Chandler's novel but not, because of institutional constraints, in the film.

These prohibitions specifically effect the subtextual discourse in certain respects, but they certainly do not exhaust it. The excess is an expression of the fact that the 'scene of the crime' bears the marks of the Uncanny, and the Uncanny is unsettling because it represents simultaneously the familiar and the unfamiliar, the reassuring and the threatening. In a patriarchal order, these qualities become literally *embodied* – the threat of femininity is represented by the desire and the fear evoked by the body of the mother. The trouble, the disturbance, at the heart of *The Big Sleep* is its symptomatic articulation of the threat posed to the law of patriarchy by the feminine. The text's response is to recuperate pleasure and reassurance through closure, but at the same time to hint at obsession and violence where closure threatens to fail.

5

A moral subject: the VD propaganda feature

In the last chapter, it was argued that on one level a film's textual operations are understandable as effects of its contexts of production. The method employed was an investigation of text/context relations in one film through exploring operations of censorship within it. The essay which follows takes up both these concerns – relations of text and context, and censorship – approaching them through new subject matter and from a different angle.

This work forms part of a larger piece of research, which was motivated by an interest in certain problems of theory and methodology in the study of cinema. Traditionally, most historical – and probably all sociological – investigations of cinema have tended to assume that films in some sense reflect what is going on outside them in the 'real world' of social structures, institutions and historical conjunctures. The chapters in this book, on the other hand, are grounded in the premiss that all representations are productive in their own right: that they construct meanings through their own particular codes and conventions. Processes of meaning production are usually investigated under the rubric of semiotics, the study of language and signification in society. Although semiotics has made some very productive inroads in the study of cinema, it does run the risk, in taking texts as its object, of forgetting that meanings are also produced in particular times and places. Just as films cannot be regarded as mere effects of historical moments or relations of production, neither on the other hand can they be read as if the meanings available from them were innocent of social, cultural and historical formation.

The semiotics of cinema and the history and sociology of film have constituted their shared object – cinema – in entirely different ways, adopting diverse methodologies for studying that object. The theoretical and methodological issues which occupy a central place in the thinking behind this essay in effect reframe the text/context problem raised in the previous one. The quest here is both for a unitary approach to theorising relations of text and context in the study of film and for a method of investigating such relations in particular institutional and historical instances.

Such a project presents a number of difficulties. Its theoretical/methodological goals, for example, are impossible to achieve *a priori* – in advance of work on concrete instances, that is. Even if this were possible, it would in any case seem – given the currently rather over-theorised state of film studies – undesirable to proceed solely at such an abstract level. The strategy adopted, therefore, has been to look closely at a historical moment, an institutional practice, or some other concrete instance. The present chapter starts by looking at a particular group of films – fiction features dealing with venereal disease – produced at a certain period. In these films, questions of sexuality and morality are raised through an attention to the fitness and integrity of the body. It is argued that these films construct spectators as 'moral subjects': but that when considered both in relation to the state of the cinema industry at the time the films were made and in conjunction with various contemporary discursive and institutional practices surrounding VD, this process involves such a degree of complexity and contradiction as to make it impossible to regard the films as simple effects of their moment of production.

There are problems involved in writing any history which eschews simple determinism or linear causality. Not least among these is the question of where to begin, how to construct an account that can handle the complexity of the various relations at work even in one instance. The written text imposes a linearity which may well do violence to the ideas expressed in it. While the methodology sought as an objective of this project ought, ideally, to emerge through the writing itself, that writing also bears the rather inconsistent burden of describing a series of events, telling 'what happened'. The procedure adopted here has been to start with film texts (Part I), and to move outward to their immediate contexts of production (Part II) towards questions of the broader social/historical context (Part III). Each of these levels, though, is intertwined with, folds back on, the other in a way that a text with a beginning, a middle and an end easily effaces.

This study aims to show how, in one particular instance, cinema – as both representation and institution – participates in the construction of social discourses; to indicate that while films may 'speak' their historical moment, they always do so in their own ways, in processes mediated by cinematic representation as autonomously productive of meaning; and that there is always space for contradiction or at least 'lack of fit' between the various levels at which discourses are produced and circulated in society. This final chapter might appear more 'scholarly' in its approach than the other contributions to this book, but it does share with them certain aspirations. For example, it takes up the task of investigating and deconstructing, with a view to understanding, culturally dominant representations, pushing such an enterprise firmly onto the terrain of the 'concretely' social and historical. It also offers itself as a contribution to an ongoing debate within film and media studies as to the status of historical investigation in these fields. But the solutions, if any, it offers to the problem of conceptualising the relationship between cinema and society are far from simple.

During and in the years immediately following World War I, there appeared in Britain a number of feature narrative films concerning themselves with 'social problems'. The problems they dealt with are quite specific: questions of morality – specifically of sexual morality – are raised via an attention to the body, its fitness, its integrity. The films were considered at the time important enough to be given a generic title: by 1919, they had come to be known as 'propaganda' – sometimes as 'health propaganda' – films. The contexts of production and exhibition of these films, their reception, the ways in which their themes are dealt with in cinematic terms – all embody a series of operations through which, at a particular moment, social discourses centring on morality, sexuality, health and nationhood were being constructed and circulated. An examination of propaganda films and their contexts, then, may shed light on how cinema, as both institution and regime of representation, participates in social processes of discursivity.

The body in question in propaganda films is primarily sexual. The sexual body is held, at the same time, to be peculiarly vulnerable – to sexual exploitation and disease, in particular. In an era of ascendancy of institutions of 'public morality' and 'public health',[1] both sexual morality and the sexual body are regarded as questions of pressing social concern – exactly as public, as opposed to private, matters: hence the self-proclaimed objective of propaganda films of bringing important issues before the public. This they did through stories about such topics as birth control, illegitimacy, prostitution and the white slave traffic. Foremost among the themes of propaganda films, though, was venereal disease. During the late 1910s especially, a number of feature films about VD were made – with such titles as *Damaged Goods* (GB, Samuelson Productions, 1919), *End of the Road* (US, Public Health Films, 1918), *Fit to Fight* (US, Public Health Films, 1919), *Open Your Eyes* (US, Warner Brothers, 1919), *The Spreading Evil* (US, John S. Lawrence, 1918). These films were often exhibited in commercial cinemas, and all of them were – or at least proclaimed themselves to be – educational. They were made, said their proponents, in order to inform the public about the nature, incidence and consequences of venereal disease. Supporters of such 'propaganda' argued first and foremost that knowledge about these matters was a good thing in itself. It followed from this that a dissemination of knowledge might help towards solving what was regarded as a grave problem for the nation: one in seven of the population, it was estimated, was affected by venereal disease (see below, Part III).

I

Given the informational function claimed for propaganda films, that they happen to be fictional narratives is worthy of note: in cinema, fiction and information are often regarded as mutually exclusive. Although the term 'documentary' was not applied to cinema before the late 1920s, films which would now be called by that name had existed since the earliest years of the medium. Indeed, during the period under consideration here, documentaries about VD ('lecture films', as they were called) were in fact being made, but these were for use in highly circumscribed non-public contexts – in army training, for instance. The films which came to attract attention under the generic label of 'propaganda' were all fictional narratives aimed, on the whole, at relatively large sections of the population.

The medium of narrative fiction and the objective of public availability are united in specific ways in the instance of the VD propaganda film. In that instance, cinema as a body of film texts intersects, with particular consequences, cinema as a set of institutions for their production, distribution and exhibition. By the late 1910s, the programme of the average commercial cinema consisted typically of at least one fiction feature film of at least an hour in length, usually with the addition of shorts – 'topicals', newsreels, travelogues, and so on. The major attraction, though, was the feature. The twin cornerstones of a rapidly developing new industry were a specific product and mode of consumption: narrative films exhibited in purpose-built cinemas.

It was in this period, then, that the fiction film and particular approaches to cinematic narration began to establish themselves as central to the entire institution of cinema. If fictional narrative was the chosen medium for VD propaganda films, the choice was a strategic one – even if not always consciously so, and not always with the results allegedly intended. Within the institution of cinema, a place already existed – together with an audience and an apparatus of reception – for narrative films. At the same time, a spectatorial apparatus, a mental machinery through which spectators could engage with, be drawn into, films, was also being set in place. Narrativity – cinematic narrativity – structured this spectatorial apparatus in particular ways, and cinema audiences were constructed through their relations, as spectators, with the ways in which stories were told in films. The physical circumstances of film reception are crucial in this process: cinema buildings already existed and were rapidly increasing in numbers. The pleasure of film spectatorship could be secured at small cost by large sectors of the population. It is generally accepted that children and the working classes were especially attracted by this new form of entertainment.

Although such a project was not without its contradictions, the VD propaganda film constitutes an attempt to capitalise on certain aspects of this situation. The objective was to produce films of a sort that might be seen in ordinary, commercial cinemas, and so be accessible (in all senses of the word) to a large audience. In the end, though, propaganda films seem to have occupied something of a marginal position in relation to the mainstream of cinema. This is for reasons having to do partly with the nature of the stories offered in them, partly with certain institutional constraints upon their accessibility, and to some extent also with the broader social and historical contexts within which the films were produced and marketed. Taken together, these conditions produce a specific mode of address for the films, a mode of constructing spectators as 'moral subjects' of a particular kind. Such an address marks the VD propaganda film as organised according to a logic in certain respects tangential to that of the mainstream cinema into which it attempted, at a certain moment, to insert itself.

The stories of VD propaganda films are in general quite

explicit in moral tone and content.[2] They appear to embody certain defining features of 'classic realist' narrative: notably an enigma-resolution structure, with conflicts worked out through the actions of fictional characters and in these characters' relations with one another. Where they depart from the classic model, perhaps, is in that characters are as a rule constructed not as psychologically-rounded individuals, but as representatives, if not of social types, certainly of moral positions. Moral position is constructed in terms of characters' sexual practices and placement in relation to discourses around the body and its health. Within the fiction, certain of these practices and discourses become privileged over against others.

Thus the film *Open Your Eyes*, for example, centres on three young men who decide to sow their wild oats. They all get syphilis. One goes to a quack for a cure, marries and has a child born blind. The second goes to a quack and gives the disease to a woman friend. The third goes to a qualified doctor and is cured. The second man intends to marry another girl, but the wedding is stopped (for altruistic reasons) by his syphilitic woman friend, who herself undergoes a cure at the hands of the qualified doctor and marries the third man.[3] In stories of this sort, characters are defined almost completely in terms of their actions: they are what they do. In this particular narrative, what characters do is posited as having clear and straightforward social consequences. Sex of a certain kind leads – inexorably, it seems – to venereal disease. Consulting a quack leads equally inexorably to the spread of infection. Consulting a qualified medical practitioner is thus the only sure way of reinstating the integrity of the diseased body, and consequently of restoring equilibrium to the world of the fiction and securing narrative closure.

Fit to Fight has a similar story, this time involving five young men:

> 'Billy, a college football man; Chick, another rich and rather dissipated college boy; Kid, a pugilist who has lost his title by weakness due to too

much drinking, promiscuous association with
women, and late hours; Hank, an ignorant
country boy who is leaving his country home and
rustic parents to seek his fortune in the city; and
Jack, a sporting cigar salesman.'[4]

As America enters World War I, this cross-section of class
types and moral positions finds itself drafted into the army.
All the men receive instruction on venereal disease from
their company commander, and each responds to the
message according to type.

On leave in town, four of the young men are picked up
by prostitutes, Billy being the only one to resist temptation.
'After this evening, Kid, impressed by the army regulations,
takes prophylaxis.' So does Jack, who nevertheless still
contracts syphilis, as also does Hank. Billy and Kid alone
escape infection. 'The picture ends with Billy and Kid
happily leaving for the war front. Back in the hospital are
the "useless slackers" who through weakness and disobedi-
ence of orders have made themselves a burden upon the
government by contracting a venereal disease.' The message
is clear: clean living is the one sure way of securing the
physical integrity necessary in order to fight for your
country. Contracting VD saps the fibre of the fighting forces
and is profoundly unpatriotic. Again, the points are made
by contrasting the actions of characters constructed as
occupying different moral positions.

This equation of bodily health, moral fibre and fighting
fitness applies exclusively to male characters, however.
Unlike *Open Your Eyes* and *Fit to Fight*, *The End of the Road* is
aimed at female audiences, though once again the actions
and the fates of different characters are counterposed. In
this story, two girls grow up together in a small town.

'One girl has the right kind of mother who has
met her child's inquiries as to the beginning of life
with truth. . . . The other girl's mother . . . has
ambitions she has never been able to gratify, and
whose one idea for her daughter is that she shall
make a rich match. . . .'

Both young women move to New York, one taking up nursing, the other obtaining employment in a department store. The nurse, 'strengthened by principle and high ideals', refuses a man's advances. The shop assistant, however, accepts the sexual attentions of a man who has no intention of marrying her, so taking her first step on 'the road that leads in the end to disease, desertion and disgrace'. She contracts syphilis. The good girl becomes an army nurse and in the course of her work comes into contact with prostitutes and 'amateurs' in the vicinity of an army camp.

The contrast in moral position posed between the two female characters motivates sequences within the film which the plot synopsis suggests are probably documentary or semi-documentary in nature. By way of a lesson, the 'bad girl' is shown exhibits of cases of advanced syphilis. The nurse's work situation motivates a description of preventative measures, emphasising the way in which police and social workers may 'save girls and boys from unwise conduct, dangerous to health and morals'. In this film, the disparity in moral position between the two main characters is explained in terms of their personal and familial histories, notably their relationships with their mothers. As far as women are concerned, the emphasis is on education, knowledge and prevention – prevention not of infection so much as of sexual activity itself. In a film aimed at women audiences, it is chastity which is presented as the one sure way to avoid disease – and disgrace: for active sexuality, disease and disgrace together lie in wait on the only other road open to women.

A range of narrative resolutions is being posed in these examples of the VD propaganda film. Each represents a particular position on venereal disease, its prevention, its containment. For women, all sexual activity, for men, promiscuous sexual activity, are dangerous. Abstaining from sex out of its 'proper' context of marriage and family is the one sure way of avoiding infection for both women and men: though once the damage is done, cure is possible (though for women, 'disgrace' is still unavoidable). But cure is not an easy route, either: it can be guaranteed only if sufferers are willing to place themselves in the hands of the right kind of professional person, submitting themselves to an authoritative medical and/or moral discourse. Characters in these stories trace their progress along a circumscribed set of routes through the limited moral positions available to them, at once embodying and reconstructing them. What all the VD victims have in common, though, is that whatever position they adopt, they suffer a specific – and narratively crucial – lack of knowledge. VD propaganda films narrativise the process through which characters' (and, presumably, spectators') eyes are opened to knowledge, and therefore to the 'truth'.

In this sense, different VD propaganda film narratives share a quality which may be taken as evidence of a common underlying structure. The initial problem in the fictional world – the rupture that sets the story in motion – is a lack: in this case, of knowledge. Had protagonists been aware of the salient facts about venereal disease and its prevention, and had they taken this knowledge to heart before embarking on the narrative road of disease and disgrace, there would, we may infer, have been no story to tell. Their ignorance, wilful or otherwise, is consequently in a way fortunate. It serves precisely to justify the project of VD propaganda in general and of VD propaganda films in particular: to inform and educate the audience, the public, who are addressed as occupying a precisely identical position of ignorance and moral corruptibility as characters in the fiction. What these narratives propose, and indeed construct, therefore, is a lack. At the same time, the fictional construction of a lack implies a promise that the lack will be filled, that the story's resolution will deliver the knowledge that was missing at the beginning.

Damaged Goods is a case in point. This 1919 British film is based on a play of the same name by Eugène Brieux which had enjoyed considerable success in the West End theatre during the early years of the War. George Dupont, soon to be married to Henriette Louches, discovers that he has contracted syphilis in a casual sexual encounter. He consults a professional practitioner who tells him that a cure will take three or four years and that he must not under any circumstances marry during that time. But his wedding is imminent, and because he can find no excuse for such a long delay, George takes the advice of a quack who promises a cure within six months. The consequences of George's precipitate marriage are explored: Henriette has a baby, which is discovered to be suffering from the disease. The family consequently finds out what George has been concealing from them – that he is syphilitic – and Henriette leaves him. He undertakes a proper cure, however, and three years later is reunited with his wife and child. The story of the woman who infects George is also told in some detail: as an employee in a couture house, she is raped by her boss and sacked when found to be pregnant. By the time George meets her, she has embarked on a career of prostitution in order to pay for her baby's upkeep in an orphanage.

The story in this film differs to some extent from the others described, mainly in its treatment of characters' sexual practices and moral positions. Like the other films, though, it is constructed around a lack of knowledge, notably on the part of George, his mother and his father-in-law. Indeed, virtually all of the characters apart from the doctor are represented as ignorant or misinformed about VD in some significant respect. The doctor, whose role it is to rectify this situation, is in consequence placed as central, both for the film's other characters and also for its audience, to the production of the absent knowledge. If the film promises to remedy a lack of knowledge, then, it is through the doctor that such a remedy is to be secured. The doctor is constituted as enunciator: provider of knowledge and speaker of truth.

The 'educational' project of VD propaganda features is, then, to narrativise the process of acquiring information and knowledge. The fictional narrative form solicits a specific kind of involvement in this process on the spectator's part. Whereas, say, a direct address documentary film would implicate the spectator in a didactic rhetoric – the 'facts' would be presented in voice-over, the image would illustrate and thus verify the content of the voice-over[5] – the fiction film demands a rather less direct mode of address. In classic realist narrative, the spectator may, for example, identify with characters and their fates. However, the narratives of VD propaganda films conform only partially to the classic model, which means that where identification with the fiction is solicited, characters occupy a rather different place within such identification. At this point, the specificity of *cinematic* storytelling intersects the moral positions constructed by VD propaganda films.

At the time these films were produced, a particular set of conventions for telling stories by means of the moving image was becoming established as the 'correct' way of making films. Within these conventions, narrative space and time are constructed in certain ways in the cinematic image, largely by means of a particular practice of editing. The continuity system involves rules for matching shots on action; matching the direction of characters' eyelines; punctuating temporal ellipses in the story; and constructing a dissected fictional space as intelligible to the spectator by staying on one side of 'the line' (the 180-degree rule) and by mapping changes in angle of view with the minimum confusion of narrative space (the 30-degree rule). By 1920, continuity editing was more or less accepted as the only proper and competent way of putting together fiction films.[6] Many films made around this period, though, bear traces of an unevenness in the application of the continuity system: or, less teleologically perhaps, these films are often marked by practices of cinematic narration which are not in fact governed by the continuity system.

In this context, it is of interest to note that in 1919 *Damaged Goods* was regarded as rather 'old-fashioned' in its style[7] : and indeed the film does look as if it could easily have been made at least four or five years earlier. Many of its scenes are constructed in frontal 'tableau' shots of the kind favoured in early cinema,[8] though a tableau-like framing and composition of shots does still remain in many films even into the 1920s. By about the mid-1910s, however, the tableau was functioning basically to establish the space of a particular scene. Within a scene, there would be cut-ins to narratively significant detail and to closer framings – such as two-shots and individual close-ups – of characters. Initially at least, however, close shots of these kinds rarely involved much change in angle of view. The formal construction of *Damaged Goods* operates very much along these lines. Silent cinema, moreover, without the resource of synchronous sound (though, given the regular performance of live musical accompaniment in the theatre, rarely in its time really 'silent'), dealt with characters' speech by a combination of expressionistic acting and written intertitles.

This combination of non-dissected narrative space with extradiegetic sound, a minimum of dialogue, and a maximum expressivity of emotion through gesture and facial expression on the part of characters/actors, is undoubtedly associated with the types of stories and modes of narration prevalent in silent cinema: notably the simple, almost folktale-like melodramas involving 'good' and 'bad' characters constructed as such through an iconography of costume, *mise-en-scène* and gesture. The camera tends to keep a distance from the action, sustaining a single angle and point-of-view even where a close-up or cut-in signals significant detail or emotion. A close-up of an actor's face, on which emotions are writ large, marks a particularly dramatic moment, especially when underlined by musical accompaniment to the scene. Intertitles function to explain action, to quote dialogue, even to comment on action or character.

VD propaganda features stand in a rather uneasy relation with contemporary approaches to cinematic narrativity. On the one hand, their construction of characters in terms of moral positions – specifically their counterposing, as moral types, of sexually active women and promiscuous men with the chaste and pure of both sexes – may be regarded as characteristic of such approaches. In this sense, their stories are indeed simple enough moral tales. At the same time, though, the films' simplicity as regards the moral positions they produce is overdetermined by the more fundamental imperative of rectifying a lack of knowledge. For instance, while codes of (say) iconography and music may construct a particular character as morally deficient, the narrative's drive towards knowledge will tend to position that character not as 'bad' but merely as ignorant or misinformed. Thus in *Damaged Goods*, for example, George – despite his moment of 'dangerous sexuality' – is presented not as depraved, but rather as a confused young man who has come up against a moral and familial impasse because of his (admittedly rather wilful) ignorance of the true horror of venereal disease. His stricken conscience and moral indecisiveness are emphasised in many an anguished close-up.

What is happening in a film such as *Damaged Goods* is that, in narrative and cinematic terms, the various moral positions set against one another are in effect subsumed to the narrative's project of dealing with a lack of knowledge. In this film, the doctor, as representative and enunciator of the desired knowledge, occupies a peculiarly privileged position. In the scenes in which he appears, he functions as a central motivator of both image and intertitles. When not shown as part of a setting (surgery, laboratory) connoting status and specialised knowledge, this character is typically presented in individual close-up, or in medium two-shot alongside whichever character is at the moment receiving the benefit of his wisdom. Everything about this man's appearance and expression conveys rectitude, sternness, strictness and rigorously unbending correctness. From this elevated position, his enunciation of information – 'the facts' about VD – acquires a peculiarly authoritative quality, as do his instructions and injunctions to other characters (urging George to break off his engagement, for instance) and his more sweepingly universalistic statements ('It is the future of the race I am defending'). He also has a great deal more to say than any of the other characters. Parts of his speeches, taken verbatim from the play on which the film is based, appear in intertitles of great length.

To the extent that knowledge is not spoken, as it were, from the film itself but is mediated through a character within the fiction, the rhetoric of the VD propaganda feature does eschew the didacticism of a direct address to the spectator. At the same time, though, the specifically cinematic aspects of characterisation may operate to some extent to subvert the fictional rhetoric. So, for example, the doctor in *Damaged Goods* functions simply and solely as repository of a knowledgeability and moral rectitude which are first of all reduced to one another, and then expressed in a degree of verbosity which stretches to the limit the capacity of silent cinema to deal with words as opposed to actions and emotions. In this film, too, a discourse outside and above any of its characters occasionally breaks through the bounds of the fiction in intertitles offering comments upon the action: 'The woman alone pays', 'The sins of the fathers', for instance – referring respectively to Edith's problems as an unmarried mother and to George's subsequent sexual encounter with her. In this sense, the film does at moments speak directly to the spectator. The contemporary reviewer who noted (with something different in mind) that 'the hygienic aspect of *Damaged Goods* is in conflict with the merely moral aspect'[9] had inadvertently hit upon a significant feature of the film's address.

In line with their avowed project of disseminating information about sexually transmitted diseases, then, VD propaganda films at once propose a want of knowledge and offer themselves as a means of filling the gap by providing not merely knowledge, but knowledge of exactly the right kind. Knowledge, though, is never innocent, nor is its source contingent. The 'correct' knowledge is presented as being of a particular kind, coming from – spoken from – a particular source. In the case of VD propaganda, knowledge is provided by Science, specifically by Science harnessed to discourses of medicine and social purity and institutionalised within practices of Public Health. It is here that the 'correct' knowledge about VD is produced, to be enunciated through the authoritative agency, on the one hand, of properly qualified medical practitioners and, on the other, of professionals whose brief was public morality – social workers.

Thus both *Open Your Eyes* and *Damaged Goods*, for example, are at pains to make distinctions between 'proper' and 'non-proper' knowledge with regard to venereal disease, and to establish a source for the former: the qualified medical practitioner as opposed to the quack. But Science and morality intersect, and the films also operate within, appeal to, a particular moral universe: the benefits of proper medical and scientific knowledge are represented as by no means easy to come by for the VD sufferer. If George Dupont in *Damaged Goods* has to wait three or four years to be cured, this may be regarded both as adequate punishment, and as sufficient restitution, for his sexual transgression. Nor perhaps is it by chance that, in the medico-moral discourse of VD propaganda, cure and salvation are repeatedly conflated. In a particularly illuminating exchange, George pleads with the doctor:

> 'No, no, for pity's sake! You can cure me before
> that. Science can do everything!'

To which the doctor sternly replies:

> 'Science is not God Almighty (except by prayer).
> The age of miracles is past.'

Despite the refusal to equate Science with God or with miraculous cures, the parenthetical reference to prayer does appeal to a concept of salvation: salvation brought about by one's own efforts as much as by either the munificence of the Almighty or the blessings of scientific knowledge. Other metaphors of salvation are evoked, too, in VD propaganda films: in *The End of the Road*, for example, social workers and police are the holders of the proper knowledge and authority to enable them to 'save girls and boys from unwise conduct, dangerous to health and morals'.

The narratives of VD propaganda films may therefore be regarded as constructing and recirculating discourses centred on knowledges of specific kinds, with particular institutional locations. In participating in the discursive and institutional construction of Public Health, these films are authorising – literally giving authority to – Science as a means of securing the health of the public – of the social, as much as of the sexual, body. At the same time, though, the power of

Science and the rewards of moral virtue are constituted as mutually dependent. The health of the sexual body serves in some respects as a metaphor for the fitness and moral soundness of the social body. In VD propaganda films this is expressed as a concern in particular with the integrity of the family in society.

Thus in *Damaged Goods*, and to a certain extent also in *Open Your Eyes*, the virulent contagiousness of VD is set up as a direct and ever-present threat – not only within the area of illicit and 'dangerous' sexual practices, but also to that sphere *par excellence* of clean and socially acceptable sex, marriage and the family. In *Open Your Eyes*, the man who goes to a quack to be cured of syphilis and then marries has a child born blind. This affliction of the family, we may infer, is a direct result of, if not a punishment for, his failure to seek knowledge in the right place and so obtain a proper cure for his disease. A similar fate befalls the Dupont family in *Damaged Goods*: there is a suggestion not only that George's wife and child are infected with syphilis, but that the baby's wetnurse is in danger of contracting it as well. 'The sins of the fathers' (somewhat obliquely referred to at the point when George meets Edith, the prostitute) have clearly come home to roost within the family. Again, moral and medical discourses are elided. In a cut-in close-up of a Biblical extract, reference is made once more to sin:

> 'Against thee, thee only have I sinned . . . be
> clear when thou judgest.'

If the integrity of the family is to be restored, both the disease and the sin must be purged.

The last scene of *Damaged Goods* marks the end of George's three-year cure and expiation. In an emblematic instance of closure for narrative cinema, George, Henriette and the child are reunited, while the doctor proclaims: 'Whom God hath joined, let no man put asunder'. In the film's closing moment, George holds the child in one arm, puts the other around his wife, and kisses both of them. If George's disease and failure to have it cured are brought about by a lack of knowledge which results in the breakup

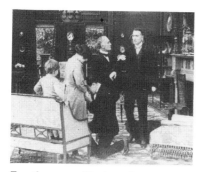

Family reconciliation: doctor at centre, standing

of his family, a full restoration of the situation and a
resolution of the film's narrative must entail a cure of the
disease and a reconciliation of the family. Both are brought
about through the doctor's agency as repository of proper
knowledge, and sealed by his positively priestly blessing.

If the 'family romance' has been a staple of narrative
cinema from its earliest years,[10] the VD propaganda film
picks up on this concern to the extent that it constructs, quite
literally, stories around heterosexual courtship, sex, marriage
and family life. The specificity of such films, however,
would be their proposal of 'improper' sexual conduct and
ensuing physical disorder as a particular kind of threat to
the integrity of the family. In this respect they depart
somewhat from the characteristic 'family romance' of
mainstream cinema. Other VD propaganda films, however,
forgo the 'family romance' altogether, thus placing themselves at yet greater distance from the core preoccupations
of mainstream narrative cinema. The theme of *Fit to Fight*,
for example, is not so much the integrity of the family as
that of the nation, as represented by its fighting forces, in
time of war. To this extent, the film participates in particular
ways in discourses circulating in contexts outside cinema
itself, discourses produced through other representations
and institutions (see Part III). The passage across discursive
contexts is by no means unproblematic or without contradiction, however. In this film, moral positions are constructed
around the contrast between men who are fighting fit

because they do not have VD, and 'useless slackers' infected by disease and in consequence unable to go to the Front. However, the possibility that, for the audience at which the film was aimed, a choice between syphilis on the one hand and possible death in the trenches on the other might not have seemed entirely attractive might be seen to introduce an element of instability into the reception of this fiction film as a piece of instruction. One thing which *is* abundantly clear in *Fit to Fight*, though, is that it is women, or women of a certain kind, who are at the root of the trouble: the soldiers are urged by their officer to 'keep away from prostitutes as the only sure way of avoiding a venereal disease'.

A preoccupation with the troublesome consequences of certain manifestations of female sexuality is in fact something of a mark of the VD propaganda film. In *The End of the Road*, for instance – as befits a film aimed at a female audience – the moral lesson appeals to a 'woman's point of view'. The background and circumstances of the fall of the 'bad girl' are explained before the inexorable consequences of disease, desertion and disgrace ensue. Similarly – and significantly, given the character's marginality in the original play – Edith's story of seduction and desertion is told at some length in the film version of *Damaged Goods*. This betokens a certain fascination with the moment of a woman's fall from sexual innocence to disgrace (there being no intermediary possibilities posed), evident also in much mainstream fiction cinema of the period. Women are constructed as essentially pure and innocent, but infinitely morally corruptible: once initiated into extramarital sex, disgrace inevitably follows. It is almost as if, in the VD propaganda film, it is the sexual initiation as much as the disease itself that brings about a woman's downfall. In a film like *The End of the Road*, the only effective way proposed for women to avoid such a downfall is foreknowledge: armed with proper sex education and high moral principles gained from her mother, the 'good girl' avoids a terrible fate and is thus able, in her capacity as a nurse, to be of service to society. Later, it is implied, she in her turn will be a good wife and mother.

VD propaganda films, with whatever degree of sympathy,

construct sexually active women as the major cause of venereal infection. This is effected within a set of discursive constructions of female sexuality which operate to distinguish it from male sexuality. Women are fundamentally innocent, but extremely vulnerable to corruption at the hands of men. At the moment of corruption, though, women immediately lose all innocence and become dangerous – to themselves as well as to men. Men, on the other hand, are not basically pure and innocent, neither are they automatically disgraced by sexual initiation. Sex in an 'improper' – that is, a non-marital – context may involve risks of other kinds for them, though: but these can be avoided by abstinence ('clean living') or reduced by a proper regard for medical expertise.

Discourses around female and male sexuality are constructed through VD propaganda films in their deployment of certain cinematic signifiers and modes of narrativity operating across other contemporary variants of fiction cinema: these include, for example, codes of characterisation and a narrativisation of female innocence and its ever-threatened loss. At the same time, though, these representations draw upon and recirculate contemporary social discourses which operate also outside of cinema *per se*. Similar arguments may be advanced concerning representations of the family both within and outside contemporary cinema, and also – though perhaps less straightforwardly – about discourses on nationhood, on the health, soundness and integrity of 'the race'.[11] What this indicates is that an exclusive attention to film texts, though productive, does not necessarily exhaust analysis of the processes by which social discourses around morality, health and nationhood are circulated in VD propaganda features: for such discourses do not inhabit films alone. A move outward from the text, then, should serve both to amplify – and perhaps also to specify and qualify – the findings of a text-based analysis.

II

When *Damaged Goods* was previewed to the film trade late in

1919, the occasion – which included a luncheon and speeches by various notables – provided, among other things, an opportunity to contrast the achievements of British cinema with those of an already hegemonic American film industry. A Member of Parliament compared the film favourably with a recent American offering on the same topic (probably *The End of the Road*), suggesting that where 'the American production dealt with the subject in all its ugliness and almost vulgarity', the British film was distinguished by 'its artistic qualities and the display of taste.'[12] Although a distinction between the vulgarity of American cinema and the tastefulness of the home product has repeatedly been appealed to in defence of British cinema, it has a particular significance in this instance.

The MP's criticism of the American film is no doubt a reference to its explicit representation of the 'horrors' of VD as set out in one of its quasi-documentary sequences: probably where the 'bad girl' is shown exhibits of cases of syphilis. This shock tactic – which was not confined to a single film, but seems to have become a mark of the entire genre of VD propaganda – suffered a good deal of contemporary condemnation. The *Times* review of *The End of the Road*, for instance, characterises one or two incidents in the film as 'revolting', while a review of the same film in the Association of Social and Moral Hygiene's journal *The Shield* suggests that the horrors of VD had already been pressed too much.[13] Another American film, *Open Your Eyes*, was similarly criticised. Photographs of the effects of diseases, says one reviewer, 'cultivate an unhealthy taste for horrors', and appeal to a 'public taste for dwelling on horrors and disease, a morbid taste fostered by the war'.[14]

By contrast with the sensationalism of the American VD films, *Damaged Goods* aimed to sell itself as a piece of 'quality' cinema: not simply on grounds of its restrained treatment of delicate subject matter, but also perhaps because it had been adapted from a stage play and consequently had aspirations to 'high art'. At the same time, though, the film was regarded as lacking in precisely those qualities which would make it 'good' cinema: 'from the point of view of screen art', says one reviewer, 'it is not good'.[15] It fails artistically, according to this writer, because it does not exploit the visual potential of cinema: specifically, its points are made in the subtitles and not in the pictures. In abstaining from the sensationalism of actually showing the horrors of VD on the screen, then, *Damaged Goods* laid itself open to accusations of failure as 'screen art'. The conclusion must be that VD propaganda films which do convey their message via the image, despite their alleged vulgarity, were to be considered better cinema because they exploited the possibilities of cinematic representation more fully, and so came closer to realising the potential of cinema as a medium of expression.

All this is relevant to the question of what VD propaganda features were intended to do, by whom, and for whom. It is clear that they were promoted in terms of their educative value: and in textual terms they do indeed deliver on this promise to the extent that their narratives aim to rectify a certain lack of knowledge. The educational project is also institutionally implicated, though: certain VD propaganda films were taken up and promoted by social purity organisations, for instance. Particularly active in this area was the National Council for Combating Venereal Disease (NCCVD), founded by Lord Sydenham of Combe, Chair of Britain's Royal Commission on Venereal Disease.[16] *The End of the Road*, for example, was approved by the NCCVD (and, incidentally, also by the Ministry of Health). The relationship between sympathetic social purity organisations and producers of VD propaganda features is less clear, however. For example, although Lord Sydenham, in a private letter written in 1917 to the Home Secretary, expressed the sentiment that a film version of *Damaged Goods* would be a good thing,[17] there is no evidence of NCCVD backing or support for the film either during or after its production. It was undertaken, it seems, as a purely commercial venture.

VD propaganda films entered the arena of exhibition in a somewhat anomalous manner, therefore. Sometimes they were showcased at special private screenings, with attendant publicity and announcements to the effect that they were not for exhibition in commercial cinemas.[18] At the same time, though, it is clear that they were in fact shown in public cinemas as well: this is certainly true of *Damaged Goods* and *The End of the Road*, for example. However, the commercial exhibition of VD propaganda films was mediated at various levels by institutional conditions. Foremost among these were probably those imposed by institutions and practices of film censorship.

By 1920, the British Board of Film Censors (BBFC) had been in existence for seven years. It had been set up following the initiative of a group of film manufacturers and renters, who during 1912 approached the Home Secretary with a proposal for a trade-sponsored board of censors.[19] Under the Cinematograph Act 1909 (for whose implementation the Home Office was responsible), the legal right of film censorship was held by local licensing authorities – those bodies responsible for granting trading licences (mandatory under the 1909 Act) to cinema proprietors. Local authorities, free to impose any 'reasonable' conditions on cinematograph licences, could legitimately include among them provisions as to the content of films. During this early period, though, the operation of censorship was rather haphazard, and there had been one or two legal *causes célèbres* and many more complaints about the kinds of films being shown in cinemas. In light of all this, the move by the film industry to establish a form of self-regulation was undoubtedly taken with a view to forestalling action on the matter by central government.

The BBFC began its active work in the New Year of 1913, with the announcement that 'No film subject will be passed that is not clean and wholesome, and absolutely above suspicion'. But such vigilance failed to mollify the critics. Since the Board's decisions were not mandatory, local authorities could accept or ignore them as they pleased. For its effectiveness, the Board depended on the support of the local licensing authorities, support which was not immediately forthcoming. Before the year was out, renewed demands for government film censorship were already being made, and within two years or so, plans were well advanced within the Home Office for the implementation of a central censorship. The BBFC was saved only by a timely change of government and the appointment of a new Home Secretary, who took the line of attempting to persuade local authorities to involve themselves more actively in film censorship.[20] But although the Home Office had retreated from the idea of a central censorship, this did not necessarily mean it was giving its backing to the BBFC instead. Indeed, wholehearted support for the Board by the government was not to be forthcoming for several years to come. The BBFC was still on trial: it was not in fact until 1923 that the Home Office recommended that local authorities should include among their conditions for granting cinematograph licences a provision to the effect that no films without a BBFC certificate could be exhibited, unless with the express permission of the licensing authority.[21]

VD propaganda features appeared on the scene, then, during a time of intense crisis for institutions and practices of film censorship in Britain. The BBFC was struggling to establish some degree of credibility for itself, both with local authorities and with the Home Office. Its decisions about individual films were still being only randomly taken up, and there were wide local variations in censorship practices. This lack of uniformity was evidently troublesome to both the Home Office and the film industry. The Home Office, for its part, was eager not to be seen involving itself directly in matters of censorship, and so was embarrassed at receiving a number of complaints about particular films and their apparently hit-and-miss regulation. These were usually passed on to the BBFC, which nevertheless got cold feet on occasion, referring some of its more difficult problems back to the Home Office.

When propaganda films started making an impact as a genre, the BBFC was evidently placed in a quandary. In the end, the Board decided to refuse certificates *a priori* to all such films: not – significantly – on the grounds that they might be indecent, but because the cinema was, according to the Board, not a suitable place to air matters of possible controversy. In 1917, the Board had refused a certificate to a film about birth control, *Where Are My Children*, but had still felt sufficiently unsure of itself to call on the Home Office for further advice on the matter. A special viewing was arranged, a telling response from the Home Office ensuing:

> 'The Censors have hitherto considered films merely from the point of view of entertainment. If they are to be viewed as a means of inculcating morals other considerations would come in and the Board feel that they do not know what they would be led into.'[22]

In other words, the BBFC had, by 1917, already constructed a distinction between entertainment on the one hand and education on the other. A film could inhabit one or other, but never both, of these categories, and only films in the former were considered suitable for exhibition in commercial cinemas. Cinemas were exclusively for 'entertainment' films: and entertainment films were to be neither educational nor controversial. By 1919, the Board found it necessary to send a circular letter to producers explaining its policy on propaganda features. These films, said the circular, were unsuitable for public commercial exhibition and were better viewed in halls specially taken for the purpose 'where securities could be taken for choosing the audience which are impossible in the ordinary cinema'.[23]

This discourse positions certain films outside the domain of mainstream commercial cinema, and so constructs as transparently legitimate a policy of refusing to certificate them for public exhibition. At the same time, it effectively sanctions, even privileges, particular formulas of audience and viewing context for different types of film: specifically, commercial cinemas, the filmgoing public, and 'entertainment' go hand-in-hand. The BBFC's censorship practices were geared wholly to this model of the cinematic institution: a model, moreover, endorsed by the Home Office. When, during 1917, Lord Sydenham of the NCCVD had written to the Home Secretary in support of a film of *Damaged Goods*, the 'entertainment' model of cinema was clearly already in place. Sydenham argued that 'the film would reach an audience that the play could not touch and . . . good might result'. But as far as the Home Office was concerned, the popular appeal of cinema was exactly the problem. A film outside the entertainment category could never be regarded as appropriate fare for the regular cinema audience, because

> 'the Cinema differs greatly from the Theatre: the audience is less intelligent and educated, and includes far more children and young people.'[24]

The inappropriateness of propaganda films for commercial exhibition is quite explicitly (though not, of course, publicly) justified in terms of the class (and age) composition of the cinema audience.

A policy of refusing certificates to one particular group of films may produce unexpected effects, however. In this case, it is precisely that policy which, on one level, effectively constituted propaganda films as a category apart. An institutional practice, in other words, has participated in the construction of a film genre. In this sense, censorship has obviously been productive. At the same time, within the complex total configuration of institutions and practices around film censorship during the 1910s, the policies of the BBFC – which were, as has been noted, scarcely authoritative or determining at this point – were quite capable of producing effects contradictory to those intended. For example, whatever the Board might have recommended with regard to particular films or groups of films, the power to forbid or permit their exhibition rested in the final instance with local licensing authorities: and many authorities were at this point quite prepared to ignore any recommendations the BBFC chose to make.

So, for instance, it came about that in 1919 – despite the BBFC's Home Office-backed threats of refusing certification – a film version of *Damaged Goods* was produced, evidently for commercial release. With an uncertificated film, a distributor would have to approach individual local authorities to seek permission to exhibit within particular areas. Producers, distributors or sponsors might try to impose conditions on exhibition, however. So, for example, one VD propaganda film, *The End of the Road*, was announced on its release to be available for exhibition in cinemas, but only provided no children under fourteen were present and the film was not shown alongside another feature. Advertisements for the film, too, were to be approved by its sponsor, the NCCVD. This particular film, it seems, was not even submitted to the Board of Censors.[25]

The Board's capacities for dissuading local authorities from allowing films to be publicly exhibited seem to have been quite limited. It is clear that VD propaganda features were shown in commercial cinemas up and down the country – though quite how widely it is hard to tell – even after the distribution and exhibition arms of the film trade also weighed into the fray with their own attempt to ban them.[26] For instance, in 1920, the Cinematograph Exhibitors' Association tried to persuade its members to refrain from booking *Damaged Goods*. Complaints nevertheless continued to be received about public screenings of this and other VD films, and there are reports of some local licensing authorities turning down such films, imposing special conditions upon their public exhibition, or restricting screening to specialised non-public venues such as Mechanics' Institutes.[27] In these circumstances, it is likely that where VD propaganda films were exhibited, they were shown either in public cinemas in scattered localities by special permission of local authorities in defiance of the BBFC and the more 'respectable' representatives of the film trade; or they were screened in special halls in circumstances of the sort favoured by the BBFC, perhaps under the aegis of one of the social purity organisations.

Nevertheless, despite the attraction of reaching large numbers of people, the exhibition of VD propaganda features in commercial cinemas presented something of a problem, even for their supporters within the social purity movement. In these circumstances in particular, reception becomes something of a hazardous business: given that publicity for the films and the composition of their audiences could rarely be regulated, 'intended' readings of

---

Don't Try to Pass this Off
Under the Guise of Entertainment

Box Office Analysis for the Exhibitor

The money-making possibilities of productions such as "Open Your Eyes" in certain localities are unquestioned, but an exhibitor who wants to keep up the standard of his theater should be cautious about jeopardizing a reputation for offering clean, wholesome entertainment. If you are catering to transients in a downtown district it may not matter so much, but even under such conditions it is well to think twice before giving place to a picture of social diseases.

Of course there is a chance of doing business on the special performance basis, one show for women and another for men. When a picture is handled in this manner it immediately gains a reputation of being unusually frank and in consequence is apt to attract a crowd of sensation seekers. Under all conditions be careful to exclude children.

There might be a chance of giving an advance showing of the film for an invited audience of physicians, ministers and social workers prominent in your town. Ask them to give candid opinions concerning the production as a suitable subject for public exhibition. Any favorable replies received may be utilized to advantage in your exploitation campaign.

The best material for a lobby display in a case of this kind is a collection of endorsement letters, preferably from people who are well known in your community. Then you may make something of the fact that the picture is authorized by the health authorities. Whatever the nature of your advertising, however, be sure that it makes clear the nature of the picture so that no one will visit your theater under a false impression.

Advice to American exhibitors, 1919

the films could by no means be ensured. Cinema proprietors with an eye to profit, for instance, were not above exploiting the sensation value of VD films in order to bring in audiences. Lurid publicity, restricting entry to persons above a certain age (at a time when there were no mandatory restrictions of this kind on admission to cinemas), or alternating women-only and men-only screenings, would undoubtedly have suggested an element of the forbidden to the filmgoing public. As one (anti-censorship) commentator was later to remark on observing the behaviour of cinemagoers queuing to see propaganda films, 'one has only to listen to the conversation of many of these people who believe they are going to see something frankly pornographic'[28] : 'these people' being, by implication, young and working class.

The problem with exhibiting propaganda films in commercial cinemas, though, had less to do with their actual content than with who saw them. In certain crucial respects, discourses of the BBFC, of the Home Office, even of certain sectors of the film trade, constructed cinema and its social function basically in class terms. Once a distinction between entertainment and non-entertainment cinema along implicitly class lines – in terms of the class composition of audiences, that is – had been constructed and put into circulation, it was recognised that 'intended' readings of films could not be guaranteed, most especially when the distinction threatened to break down. Since exhibiting propaganda films in commercial cinemas constituted a mixture of categories, it was obviously to be deprecated. The position of propaganda features in relation to institutions and practices of censorship is an especially important condition of their marginality in relation to mainstream cinema.

But the situation, certainly in 1919, was more contradictory than this analysis might suggest. For despite the effectivity of what may be termed discourses of categorisation, there was nevertheless a movement towards, a space opened up for, resistance to those discourses. On a very general level, for example, those very relations of power which marginalised the films with regard to mainstream cinema also, and simultaneously, constituted an incitement to discourse around their subject matter, namely sex. That is to say, there is an incitement, if not to the actual production of films on 'propaganda' topics, certainly to modes of reception of such films which would confound the 'educational' objectives of their social purity advocates.

More specifically, space for such 'resistant' readings was opened up within film texts themselves, in the deployment of strategies of narration already to some extent established in mainstream fiction cinema. In some respects, propaganda features did not differ greatly from the standard fare of commercial cinemas, and so might not have seemed widely out of place in them. On another level, though, resistance also carries institutional resonances. Erratic and sometimes antagonistic relations between the Home Office, the BBFC and local authorities provided a space for intervention, an opportunity which was grasped on one side by elements in the film trade motivated by financial gain or even social concern to produce and promote propaganda films, and on the other by social purity organisations wishing to get their message across to broad sections of the public. That the interests of these two groups did not always coincide is evident, for example, in the efforts exerted by the NCCVD to control publicity for commercial screenings of films like *The End of the Road*.

Nor indeed was there unanimity within the social purity movement itself as to the value of propaganda films. In the NCCVD, for example, disseminating information on questions of 'social hygiene' – a reference to all matters sexual – appears to have been regarded as unquestionably a good thing. This body was obviously concerned to address itself directly to the public, particularly to the working class public: its endorsement of cinema as a propaganda vehicle came about exactly because of the large, and largely working class, audience the medium could command. This, however, was precisely the basis of objection from other social purity groups, many of whom disdained cinema. This attitude had a great deal to do with the class composition of the cinema audience: but also – and relatedly – it was sometimes felt that cinema was dangerous in itself, because the conditions (darkness, proximity to strangers, and so on) in which films were viewed, not to mention the allegedly dubious content of certain films, themselves constituted moral risks. Using cinema for propaganda purposes, it was felt, might therefore turn out to be self-defeating. More specifically, the methods by which propaganda films constructed their moral messages were disputed: this is especially evident in the case of VD propaganda films' tendency to detail the 'horrors' of venereal disease. It was sometimes felt that 'constructive moral teaching' might be more effective than scaring people.[29]

As time passed, the social purity movement seems to have become increasingly wary of supporting the commercial exhibition of propaganda films, though the NCCVD (which changed its name in 1925 to the British Social Hygiene Council) steadfastly maintained its position. Even after the mid-1920s, when a degree of uniformity in censorship practices had been secured and the BBFC's decisions were now much more widely accepted by local authorities, propaganda films continued to be shown in commercial cinemas. At a certain point, indeed, this practice achieved a degree of institutionalisation: the BBFC continued to refuse certificates, but many local authorities instituted special machinery for dealing with applications to show propaganda films in their areas.[30] In a speech made in 1929, Ivor Montagu, a campaigner against political censorship of films, paints a picture of propaganda films as a thriving and profitable sideline for the film trade:

> the only films which it is possible to distribute without leave of the Board of Censors are lurid and highly-coloured melodramas, which by their very flamboyance are capable of earning tens of thousands of pounds, such as *The End of the Road* dealing with venereal disease and *The White Slave Trade*.[31]

A clear divergence of interest between the film trade on the one hand and the social purity movement on the other emerges at this point. The increasing scepticism of many elements of the latter about the commercial exhibition of propaganda films was bolstered by research and analysis, often quite sophisticated in nature. For example, in the early 1930s, one social purity organisation, the National Vigilance Association, was advised by another, the American Social Hygiene Association, that commercial exhibition of propaganda films was not a good idea 'because in spite of all possible safeguards in advance . . . it has been found that sensational publicity for advertising purposes, and the consequent opposition of certain civic and religious groups, have resulted'. The difficulty with commercial screenings lay not only with the often 'sex-exciting' character of publicity for the films, however, but also with the problem of ensuring that the films would be read for their 'social hygiene' content and not be of 'pornographic interest to their audiences'. Limits to the instability of meaning in these texts could, it was felt, be imposed only by tightly controlling the conditions of their reception. Propaganda films, then, were best shown non-commercially:

> 'under the auspices of . . . organisations interested in social hygiene, or reputable individuals. Audiences are usually selected groups. . . . [A] speaker explains and supplements the important points made in the picture.'[32]

This advice was based on the findings of a study undertaken during 1922 of audience reactions to, and effects on subsequent behaviour of, the VD propaganda film *Fit to Fight*. The researchers had questioned the utility of using fictional narrative in this type of film, stressing the significance of exhibition context and audience composition as regards their reception.[33]

Although never articulated in quite such terms, it is clear from all this that a crucial problem for social purity organisations was the instability of propaganda films as bearers of meaning. In particular their placement within, or at the margins of, institutions and textual operations of mainstream commercial cinema opened them up to unintended and probably 'undesirable' readings. Arguing against propaganda films, one social purity campaigner attributed this to the fundamentally erotic character of the pleasure of narrative cinema:

> 'instead of affecting the mind, and still less so the heart, [film dramas] affect the nerves, and, above all, the sexual instincts. . . . In that lies the mysterious secret of the astonishing success of the cinemas.'[34]

Aside from the effects of pleasures evoked in spectator–text relations in cinema, it may also be argued in the specific case of VD propaganda features that an important condition of unintended readings is precisely those practices of censorship which on the one hand marginalise the films *vis-à-vis* commercial cinema, while on the other producing special conditions for their exhibition and reception.

VD propaganda features continued to be produced long after the disappearance of the social conditions in which they first emerged at the end of World War I. They were being made and commercially exhibited at least into the late 1930s: for example, *Marriage Forbidden*, an American remake of *Damaged Goods*, was released in Britain in 1938 under the auspices of the British Social Hygiene Council. Such durability is perhaps to be explained by propaganda films' peculiar capacity to generate a variety of readings. By the 1930s, however, these films had secured their own institutional niche as well as their own 'aberrant' readings. Both transcend the conditions under which VD propaganda films made their initial appearance.

MARRIAGE
FORBIDDEN

From EUGENE BRIEUX'S FAMOUS PLAY

"DAMAGED GOODS"

Written for the Screen by UPTON SINCLAIR

———•———

Produced by PHIL GOLDSTONE	Associate Producer IRVING STARR
	Directed by PHIL STONE
Screen play by JOSEPH HOFFMAN	Art Direction, FRANK BAXTER
Recording Engineer FERL REDD	Film Editor HOLBROOK TODD

SHOWN UNDER THE AUSPICES OF THE BRITISH SOCIAL HYGIENE COUNCIL

Length 5538 ft.   ·   ·   ·   Running Time 61 mins.

Publicity for private screening, 1938

128

III

At the moment in the late 1910s when propaganda films acquired their generic title and a spate of films dealing with VD appeared, a moral panic about venereal diseases, syphilis in particular – its high incidence, its enormous contagiousness, its dreadful consequences – was raging. In 1913, a Royal Commission had been set up to look into the problem. By 1916, when the Commission's Report was published, Britain was two years into war, and the problem seemed even worse than before. It was not only that venereal disease was much more widespread than had been anticipated; according to the Royal Commission, it also had 'grave and far-reaching effects . . . upon the individual and the race'.[35] The findings of the Commission were widely publicised, and the suggestion that, as a preventative measure, 'the young should be taught to lead a chaste life as the only certain way of avoiding infection'[36] received an enthusiastic reception. VD propaganda films may thus be considered in some degree as part of an 'education for chastity' movement in Britain.

The Report of the Royal Commission on Venereal Diseases constructs a discourse on nationhood, sexuality and public morality which was to be a crucial component of the moral panic following its publication. This discourse – reconstructed, recirculated and modified across a variety of representations over several years – operates a conflation of disease with the state of the British nation, or 'the race'. Fears that the race was in decline were occasioned in part by the concrete threat posed to its integrity from without by the enemy. But overdetermining such fears were anxieties about changes in social and sexual mores, the temporary breakup of families, and the equally temporary emancipation of women, in time of war. All these are condensed in a moral panic about diseases, specifically – and not by chance – about sexually-transmitted disorders that could spread uncontrollably and have terrible social consequences. At a particular moment, then, a discursive conflation of the moral and spiritual state of the nation with its physical health, with the fitness of the national body, combines with fears about uncontained sexuality to produce a moral panic with venereal disease as its focus.[37]

VD propaganda films are not merely an effect of this moral panic, however: they participate in it, constructing, reconstructing and circulating discourses in their own right, as well as drawing upon wider social discourses. The latter is evident particularly in the concern of individual films with the threat posed by VD to the family; with the state of 'the race'; with the need for the country's fighting men to keep themselves fit in body and spirit by avoiding contagion. To the extent that these films claim to be educational, they participate also in discourses of social purity, discourses which constitute widespread knowledge about VD as a crucially necessary – if not a sufficient – condition for its control. In this particular quest for knowledge, the 'problem' is constantly invoked – as if such repetitiveness, far from participating in the construction of a moral panic, will make it go away:

> 'Continuous and consistent efforts will be required
> to keep the complex question of venereal disease
> before the public mind. . . . '[38]

In contemporary comments on VD propaganda films, as well as in the films themselves, the desirability of 'frankness' in these matters is often appealed to. These films are part of a broader incitement to sexual discourse which marks the moral panic over venereal disease of the 1910s. To this extent, they recirculate discourses in operation in media – government reports, newspapers, and so on – outside cinema itself. At the same time, though, fiction films, deploying modes of representation and address peculiar to cinema and drawing on more general codes of narrativity, mediate, modify and reconstruct these discourses in specific ways. So, for instance, VD propaganda features address their spectators as moral subjects by constructing moral positions for their fictional characters; address spectators as lacking in knowledge and promise to rectify that lack; claim to rectify the lack by constructing the acquisition of knowledge as coterminous with narrative closure, the 'happy ending'. In the course of all this, they draw on and rework on the one hand discourses of social purity, and on the other codes of narrative cinema, to position their moral subjects in certain ways: for instance, as either male or female, as occupying particular positions with regard to sexuality, sexual practices and 'dangerous sexualities'.

The morally-positioned spectators of VD propaganda films are also a social audience, however. Audiences for cinema during this period were – or were seen as – predominantly working class. It might therefore be suggested that VD propaganda films participate in the process termed by Foucault the 'moralisation of the poorer classes',[39] a pervasive deployment of sexuality as an instrument of power. Foucault argues that 'bio-power' – the constitution of the body as a site of the exercise of power – is expressed in the correlation of a 'racism of expansion' with a concern with the (sexual) body as strong, vigorous and healthy. Not only, in other words, is the health of the nation seen at once in physical and in sexual terms, but relations of class are also at stake in this process.

When it comes to considering particular instances, though, matters become rather more complex than Foucault's argument would suggest. In the case of the VD propaganda features produced just after World War I, a series of specific mediations and contradictions is in operation. First of all, the films' deployment of existing codes of narrativity and cinematic representation perhaps lends them more readily to an emphasis on the family – precisely the 'family romance' – than on the state of the race (though the two are obviously not unrelated). Thus, in this instance, the construction of discourses across particular types of fiction cinema may specify or relativise the broader relations of power implied in the notion of the moralisation of the poorer classes.

So too may the operation of specific institutional discourses, especially those surrounding the films' reception. While on the one hand VD propaganda films, as texts, may be regarded as constructing certain knowledges and the places whence they come as peculiarly authoritative, the films' reception was conditioned by institutional practices which effect their own, sometimes contradictory, readings. In combination with the films' participation in an incitement to sexual discourse, the logic of these conditions – censorship and commercial exhibition in particular – was partly to set limits on the construction of working class audiences as moral subjects along the lines apparently 'intended' by the films. But also – and especially where films were shown commercially and exploited as in a certain way 'different' because of their extraordinary conditions of exhibition and special status as objects of censorship – it was to provoke unintended, even resistant, readings.

Notes and references

Introduction

1 See, for example, Robin Blackburn (ed.), *Ideology in Social Science*, London, Fontana, 1972; Raymond Williams, 'Base and superstructure in marxist cultural theory', *New Left Review*, no.82, 1973, pp.3-16; Louis Althusser, 'Ideology and ideological state apparatuses', *Lenin and Philosophy and Other Essays*, London, New Left Books, 1971, pp.121–73.
2 *Elements of Semiology*, London, Jonathan Cape, 1967; *Mythologies*, London, Paladin, 1973.
3 These developments are traced in Rosalind Coward and John Ellis, *Language and Materialism*, London, Routledge & Kegan Paul, 1978.
4 See, for example, Mary Ann Doane *et al.*, 'Feminist film criticism: an introduction', *Re-Vision: Essays in Feminist Film Criticism*, Los Angeles, American Film Institute, 1984, pp.1-17; Annette Kuhn, 'Women's genres', *Screen*, vol.25, no.1, 1984, pp.18-28.

Chapter 1 Living dolls and 'real women'

1 This essay was first published in *Camerawork*, no.12, 1979, pp.10–11. My thanks for their support to the

women in Second Sight, especially co-authors Frances, Jill and Cassandra.

2 John Berger, *Ways of Seeing*, Harmondsworth, Penguin, 1972.

3 John Szarkowski (ed.), *E. J. Bellocq – Storyville Portraits: Photographs from the New Orleans Red Light District circa 1912*, London Scolar Press, 1978; John Kobal (ed.), *Hollywood Glamor Portraits*, London, Constable, 1976.

4 Sigmund Freud, 'The "Uncanny" ' (1919), *The Standard Edition of the Complete Psychological Works of Sigmund Freud*, London, Hogarth Press, 1953-74, vol.17, pp.219-52.

5 Royal Academy of Arts, *Post-Impressionism: Crosscurrents in European Painting*, London, RAA and Weidenfeld & Nicolson, 1979, p.64.

Chapter 2 Lawless seeing

1 On social, cultural and political consequences of these developments, see Walter Benjamin, 'The work of art in the age of mechanical reproduction', *Illuminations*, London, Fontana, 1973, pp.219-53.

2 For a discussion of these and related issues in relation to examples of early twentieth-century photography, see Allan Sekula, 'On the invention of photographic meaning', in Victor Burgin (ed.), *Thinking Photography*, London, Macmillan, 1982, pp.84-109.

3 Roland Barthes, 'The photographic message', *Image–Music–Text*, London, Fontana, 1977, pp.15-31.

4 David Hamilton and Alain Robbe-Grillet, *Dreams of Young Girls*, London, Collins, 1971.

5 Sigmund Freud, 'Analysis of a phobia in a five-year-old boy' (1909), *The Standard Edition of the Complete Psychological Works of Sigmund Freud*, London, Hogarth Press, 1953-74, vol.10, pp.1-145; 'Fetishism' (1927), *ibid.*, vol.21, pp.147-57.

6 John Berger, *Ways of Seeing*, Harmondsworth, Penguin, 1972, Ch.3.

7 For a consideration of how pinups work in one popular newspaper, see Patricia Holland, 'The page three girl speaks to women, too', *Screen*, vol.23, no.3, 1983, pp.84-102.

8 Angela Carter, *The Sadeian Woman and the Ideology of Pornography*, New York, Pantheon, 1978, Ch.1.

9 Recent feminist commentaries emphasising violent aspects of pornography include: Irene Diamond, 'Pornography and repression: a reconsideration', *Signs*, vol.5, no.4, 1980, pp.686-701; Andrea Dworkin, *Pornography: Men Possessing Women*, London, The Women's Press, 1981; Laura Lederer (ed.), *Take Back the Night: Women on Pornography*, New York, Morrow, 1980; Diana Russell and Susan Griffin, 'On pornography', *Chrysalis*, no.4, 1977, pp.11-17.

10 The existence of pornography (directed at male consumers) in which women dominate men also calls for explanation. Jessica Benjamin begins such a project by discussing the psychic functions of sadomasochistic fantasy for both sexes in 'Master and slave: the fantasy of erotic domination', in Ann Snitow *et al.* (eds), *Desire: the Politics of Sexuality*, London, Virago, 1984, pp.292-311. The relationship between sexual fantasy and pornography cannot be assumed to be either simple or direct, however. In the case of sadomasochistic pornography, certainly, further investigation of this relationship is called for.

Chapter 3 Sexual disguise and cinema

1 This chapter is developed from a talk given at a weekend event at Tyneside Cinema, Newcastle, in May 1983, 'Changing Gear'. My thanks to Sheila Whitaker for providing the opportunity to do this work, and to Mandy Merck for provoking and sharing ideas.

2 Sima Godfrey, 'The dandy as ironic figure', *Sub-stance*, no.36, 1982, pp.21-33.

3 Sandra M. Gilbert, 'Costumes of the mind: transvestism

as metaphor in modern literature', *Critical Inquiry*, vol.7, no.2, 1980, pp.391-417.

4 Roland Barthes, *The Pleasure of the Text*, New York, Hill & Wang, 1975.

5 This argument is informed by a structural approach to narrative analysis. See especially Vladimir Propp, *Morphology of the Folktale*, Austin, University of Texas Press, 1968.

6 William Luhr and Peter Lehman also make this point in ' "Crazy world full of crazy contradictions": Blake Edwards' *Victor/Victoria*', *Wide Angle*, vol.5, no.4, 1983, pp.4-13.

7 Tzvetan Todorov, 'Categories of the literary narrative', *Film Reader*, no.2, 1977, pp.19-37.

8 Tzvetan Todorov, 'The fantastic in fiction', *Twentieth Century Studies*, no.3, 1970, pp.76-92.

9 See, for example, Christian Metz, *Psychoanalysis and Cinema: the Imaginary Signifier*, London, Macmillan, 1982.

10 Laura Mulvey, 'Visual pleasure and narrative cinema', *Screen*, vol.16, no.3, pp.6-18.

11 *Ibid.*

Chapter 4 *The Big Sleep:* censorship, film text and sexuality

1 An earlier version of this chapter was presented at the Athens, Ohio, Film Conference in April 1980, and has been published under the title '*The Big Sleep*: a disturbance in the sphere of sexuality', *Wide Angle*, vol.4, no.3, 1980, pp.4-11. Thanks are due to Maxine Fleckner of the Wisconsin Center for Film and TV Research for making available for study a print of *The Big Sleep*, and to students in the Film Criticism seminar at the University of Iowa, Spring 1979.

2 *New York Times*, 24 August 1946, p.6.

3 Vladimir Propp, *Morphology of the Folktale*, Austin, University of Texas Press, 1968, p.21.

4 See, for example, Peter Wollen, '*North by Northwest*: a morphological analysis', *Film Form*, no.1, 1976. pp.19-34;

Patricia Erens, '*Sunset Boulevard*: a Proppian analysis', *Film Reader*, no.2, 1977, pp.90-5.

5 Leslie Midkiff DeBauche, '*The Big Sleep*: a morphological awakening', paper presented at seminar on Film Criticism, University of Iowa, Spring 1979. Table 4.1 is abstracted from DeBauche's essay.

6 My account of *The Big Sleep*'s production history is reconstructed from a number of sources, some more reliable than others. Where there is disagreement, I have used the most reliable: *The Big Sleep*, daily production progress reports, University of Southern California, Archives of Performing Arts; *The Big Sleep*, scripts and related material, United Artists Collection, Wisconsin Center for Film and Theater Research; George P. Garrett *et al.* (eds), *Film Scripts One*, New York, Appleton-Century-Crofts, 1971, pp.137-329; Bruce Kawin, *Faulkner and Film*, New York, Ungar, 1977; Joseph Blotner, *Faulkner: a Biography*, New York, Random House, 1974; Joseph Blotner (ed.), *Selected Letters of William Faulkner*, New York, Random House, 1977; Lauren Bacall, *By Myself*, London, Jonathan Cape, 1979; William Luhr, *Raymond Chandler and Film*, New York, Ungar, 1982.

7 Rules I.3, II.4 and VI.1 of the Production Code. See Ruth Inglis, *Freedom of the Movies: a Report on Self-regulation*, Chicago, University of Chicago Press, 1947, pp.205-19.

8 Mary Beth Haralovich and Cathy Root Klaprat, '*Marked Woman* and *Jezebel*: the spectator-in-the-trailer', *Enclitic*, vol.5, no.2/vol.6, no.1, 1982, pp.66-74; transcript of *The Big Sleep* trailer, United Artists Collection, Wisconsin Center for Film and Theater Research.

9 DeBauche, *op. cit.*

10 Sigmund Freud, 'The interpretation of dreams' (1900), *The Standard Edition of the Complete Psychological Works of Sigmund Freud*, London, Hogarth Press, 1953-74, vol.4, p.142; see also Christian Metz, *Psychoanalysis and Cinema: the Imaginary Signifier*, London, Macmillan, 1982, pp.253-65.

11 Sigmund Freud, 'The "Uncanny" ' (1919), *op. cit.*, vol.17, pp.219-52.

Chapter 5 A moral subject: the VD propaganda feature

1 See Jeffrey Weeks, *Sex, Politics and Society: the Regulation of Sexuality since 1800*, London, Longman, 1981, Ch.11.
2 Descriptions of films are based in part upon viewings made possible by the National Film Archive and by David Samuelson. I have also relied heavily on contemporary documents, published and unpublished. Unpublished material is from Home Office papers at the Public Record Office (PRO) and from the National Vigilance Association (NVA) Archive at the Fawcett Library, London. My thanks to Harold Dunham for additional information about *Damaged Goods*, and to Jane Caplan for comments on a draft of this chapter.
3 *Kinematograph Weekly*, 22 January 1920, p.119.
4 Quoted passages referring to *Fit to Fight* and *The End of the Road* are from synopses of the films in NVA Archive, file S1³.
5 Bill Nichols, 'Documentary theory and practice', *Screen*, vol.17, no.4, 1976-7, pp.34-48; Annette Kuhn, 'The camera I: observations on documentary', *Screen*, vol.19, no.2, pp.71-84. Silent films, of course, would have no incorporated voice-over, though the notion of a 'lecture film' does imply an authoritative voice, in this case external to the film – precisely that of a lecturer.
6 David Bordwell and Kristin Thompson, *Film Art: An Introduction*, Reading, Mass., Addison-Wesley, 1979, pp.163-73; Barry Salt, *Film Style and Technology: History and Analysis*, London, Starword, 1983, pp.162-5; David Bordwell, Kristin Thompson and Janet Staiger, *The Classical Hollywood Cinema: Film Style and Mode of Production to 1960*, London, Routledge & Kegan Paul, forthcoming.
7 Rachael Low, *The History of the British Film 1918-29*, London, George Allen & Unwin, 1971, p.141.
8 Noel Burch, 'How we got into pictures: notes accompanying *Correction Please*', *Afterimage*, nos 8-9, 1981, pp.22-38.
9 *Kinematograph Weekly*, 25 December 1919, p.70.
10 Stephen Heath, *Questions of Cinema*, London, Macmillan, 1981, Ch.4.

11 On the latter, see Lucy Bland and Frank Mort, 'Look out for the "good time" girl: dangerous sexualities as threat to national health', *Formations of Nation and People*, London, Routledge & Kegan Paul, 1984, pp.131-51.

12 *Kinematograph Weekly*, 25 December 1919, p.63.

13 *Times*, 8 November 1919, p.15e; *The Shield*, December 1919-January 1920, pp.189-90.

14 *Kinematograph Weekly*, 22 January 1920, p.119.

15 *Ibid.*, 25 December 1919, p.70.

16 On the social purity movement, see Jeffrey Weeks, *op. cit.*, Chs 5 and 11, *passim*; Edward J. Bristow, *Vice and Vigilance: Purity Movements in Britain since 1700*, Dublin, Gill & Macmillan, 1977. On the NCCVD, see *ibid.*, p.149.

17 PRO HO 45/10955: letter to Sir George Cave, 6 August 1917.

18 On *Open Your Eyes*, for example, see *Kinematograph Weekly*, 22 January 1920, p.119.

19 Neville March Hunnings, *Film Censors and the Law*, London, George Allen & Unwin, 1967, pp.51-2; PRO HO 45/10551: notes on a deputation, 22 February 1912.

20 PRO HO 45/10811: circular to local licensing authorities including model conditions for cinematograph licences, 24 January 1917; *Bioscope*, 1 February 1917, p.421.

21 PRO HO 158/23: circular on censorship of cinematograph films, 6 July 1923.

22 PRO HO 45/10955: Home Office report on *Where Are My Children*, 14 April 1917.

23 British Board of Film Censors, *Annual Report 1919*.

24 PRO HO 45/10955: handwritten minute, 14 August 1917.

25 *Times*, 11 November 1919, p.11d; 5 January 1920, p.10a.

26 Neville March Hunnings, *op. cit.*, p.71.

27 *The Cinema*, 16 December 1920; Rachael Low, *op. cit.*, p.61.

28 Dorothy Knowles, *The Censor, the Drama and the Film, 1900-1934*, London, Allen & Unwin, 1934, p.244.

29 *The Shield, op. cit.*, p.190.

30 See, for example, London County Council, 'Conditions under which Propaganda films may be exhibited at premises licensed by the Council', March 1926, NVA

Archive, file S1^E.

31 Ivor Montagu, 'The censorship of sex in films', World League for Sexual Reform, *Proceedings of the Third Congress, 1929*, London, Kegan Paul, Trench & Trubner, 1930, p.330.

32 Material quoted in this paragraph is from 'Memorandum on the Use of Social Hygiene Propaganda Films in the United States', 1932, NVA Archive, file S1^3.

33 Karl S. Lashley and John B. Watson, *A Psychological Study of Motion Pictures in Relation to Venereal Disease Campaigns*, Washington, US Interdepartmental Social Hygiene Board, 1922.

34 *Vigilance Record*, November 1931, p.41.

35 Royal Commission on Venereal Diseases, *Final Report of the Commissioners*, Cd. 8189, London, HMSO, 1916, para.232.

36 Edward J. Bristow, *op. cit.*, p.149.

37 Lucy Bland and Frank Mort, *op. cit.*

38 Royal Commission on Venereal Diseases, *op. cit.*, para. 236.

39 Michel Foucault, *The History of Sexuality: Volume 1, An Introduction*, New York, Pantheon Books, 1978, p.122.

Further reading

Listed below are some publications which treat central themes and issues arising throughout this book. The list is not intended to be exhaustive: more specific suggestions for further reading, especially around topics dealt with in individual essays, may be found in the Notes and References section.

Articles on relevant topics are also regularly published in such journals as *Formations* (London, Routledge & Kegan Paul), *Screen* (Glasgow, John Logie Baird Centre, University of Glasgow), and *Wide Angle* (Athens, Ohio, Athens Center for Film and Video).

Sexuality

Foucault, Michel, *The History of Sexuality: Volume 1, An Introduction*, New York, Pantheon Books, 1978.

Freud, Sigmund, 'Three essays on the theory of sexuality' (1905), in *The Standard Edition*, vol.14, pp.109-40.

Freud, Sigmund, 'Instincts and their vicissitudes' (1915), in *The Standard Edition*, vol.7, pp.123-245.

Freud, Sigmund, 'Fetishism' (1927), in *The Standard Edition*, vol.21, pp.147-57.

Freud, Sigmund, 'Female sexuality' (1931), in *The Standard Edition*, vol.21, pp.221-43.

Freud, Sigmund, *The Standard Edition of the Complete Psychological Works of Sigmund Freud*, London, Hogarth Press, 1953-74.

Heath, Stephen, *The Sexual Fix*, London, Macmillan, 1982.

Heresies Collective, *The Sex Issue*, *Heresies*, no.12, 1981.

Mitchell, Juliet and Rose, Jacqueline, *Feminine Sexuality: Jacques Lacan and the école freudienne*, London, Macmillan, 1982.

Snitow, Ann *et al.* (eds), *Desire: the Politics of Sexuality*, London, Virago Press, 1984.

Weeks, Jeffrey, *Sex, Politics and Society: the Regulation of Sexuality since 1800*, London, Longman, 1981.

Textual analysis

Barthes, Roland, *S/Z*, New York, Hill & Wang, 1974.

Barthes, Roland, *The Pleasure of the Text*, New York, Hill & Wang, 1975.

Bennett, Tony, *Formalism and Marxism*, London, Methuen, 1979.

Eagleton, Terry, *Literary Theory: An Introduction*, Minneapolis, University of Minnesota Press, 1983.

Todorov, Tzvetan, *The Poetics of Prose*, Ithaca, Cornell University Press, 1977.

The photographic image

Barthes, Roland, *Image–Music–Text*, London, Fontana, 1977.

Benjamin, Walter, 'The work of art in the age of mechanical reproduction', in *Illuminations*, London, Fontana, 1973, pp.219-53.

Berger, John, *Ways of Seeing*, Harmondsworth, Penguin, 1972.

Berger, John, *About Looking*, New York, Pantheon Books, 1980.

Burgin, Victor (ed.), *Thinking Photography*, London, Macmillan, 1982.

Spence, Jo *et al.* (eds), *Photography/Politics: One*, London, Photography Workshop, 1979.

Williamson, Judith, *Decoding Advertisements: Ideology and Meaning in Advertising*, London, Marion Boyars, 1978.

The cinematic image

Bordwell, David and Thompson, Kristin, *Film Art: An Introduction*, Reading, Massachusetts, Addison-Wesley, 1979.

Burch, Noel, *Theory of Film Practice*, London, Secker & Warburg, 1973.

De Lauretis, Teresa, *Alice Doesn't: Feminism, Semiotics, Cinema*, Bloomington, Indiana University Press, 1984.

Doane, Mary Ann *et al.* (eds), *Re-Vision: Essays in Feminist Film Criticism*, Los Angeles, American Film Institute, 1984.

Heath, Stephen, *Questions of Cinema*, London, Macmillan, 1981.

Kaplan, E. Ann (ed.), *Women in Film Noir*, London, British Film Institute, 1978.

Kuhn, Annette, *Women's Pictures: Feminism and Cinema*, London, Routledge & Kegan Paul, 1982.

Metz, Christian, *Psychoanalysis and Cinema: the Imaginary Signifier*, London, Macmillan, 1982.

Society for Education in Film and Television, *Screen Reader 2: Cinema and Semiotics*, London, SEFT, 1981.

Index

Index